Take Charge!

Take Charge!

A Manager's Guide
to Specialty Retailing

EDDY KAY

THE ARMARIUM PRESS INC.

NEW IPSWICH, NEW HAMPSHIRE

Printing History

2 4 6 8 10 9 7 5 3
First Edition
Copyright © 2003 by Eddy Kay

ISBN: 0-9707825-27

Cover design by Jean-Paul Duberg.
Cover photography by Ted Schurter.
Illustrations by Emma Stephens Larson.
Crab and butterfly woodcut by Matthew Grogan.

Printed in the United States of America.

THE ARMARIUM PRESS.
110 MOUNTAIN VIEW DRIVE
NEW IPSWICH, NEW HAMPSHIRE 03071
www.TheArmariumPress.com
www.GoodNewsAbout.com

Acknowledgments

I extend my thanks to Jennifer Seyler, S.P.H.R., for her careful review of the sections of this book that relate to employment law and human resources.

And as always, my thanks to the entire team at The Armarium Press... especially to my intrepid researchers Mark Halvorsen and Erin Mulholland for tracking down the retailers for the SPECIALIST SPOTLIGHTS... and to Jean-Paul Duberg for designing a cover that perfectly captures my belief that life as a specialist retailer should be bright, bold, and fun.

This book is dedicated to all the specialist retailers
who used to have hair.

Table of Contents

Chapter 1
It's Time to Take Charge!

Managers! They draw salaries just for hiding in an office all day waiting for trouble and are treated to catered meetings down at HQ. So, naturally, the thought uppermost in my mind when I started working the salesfloor at my first retail job was: "When do *I* get to be in charge around here?" I didn't wait long. After a formal screening process ("Eddy, you seem to understand our paperwork. Can you handle a bank deposit?"), I was promoted and handed the keys to the store.

As in many retail outfits, then and today, employees tagged as "management material" are usually promoted for reasons that have nothing to do with actual management skills. Management is not about paperwork or procedure. At heart, it is a test of your people skills: how well you're able to assemble a team of players who love to play the game — and then, how well you inspire that team to win, day after day, sales season after sales season.

We all know that the game of retailing is getting more and more competitive every day. Superstores are flying at you from every angle, and even if you're the only bookshop in a town 500 miles from the nearest Borders, Amazon is lurking just a click away.

Then there's the not-so-good news that your prospective team players are completely different today from even a decade ago. Never having lived in a world without PlayStations, many of the kids filling out employment applications completely miss the point that what makes technology magic is its departure from the real world. But whether they like it or not, your store *is* in the real world. It's not a computer game in which they're allowed to figure out the rules on their own.

Building a solid sales and support team has never been more challenging for the specialist retailer — or more important. Regardless of how your competitors or the workforce have changed, there's one bright and shining constant in the retail universe: the need for employees who can offer good, old-fashioned customer service... the kind of service that truly allows a single independent retailer to stand out from the crowd.

Happily, there's still plenty of good news in retailing these days — and you'll find much of it within the pages of this book. With real-life examples throughout and a SPECIALIST SPOTLIGHT at the end of each chapter, I'm going to teach you how to mold your employees into the kind of team that wins game after game.

You can't have your people doing what *they* think is right. They don't have a clue about how the game of specialist retailing is really supposed to be played. A team that plays by the rules — *your* rules — not only makes your life easier, but is less likely to put you out of business.

Consider Bobby Spaice, one of my most memorable employees. Spaceman would take care of his customers at any price. And he didn't care what it cost because he wasn't paying for it. A man came into our store one day looking to replace the broken dustcover (a $42 part) on his turntable (an ancient mechanical device used for spinning vinyl recordings). Bobby knew it would take about six weeks for the dustcover to arrive, so he "borrowed" one from a brand new turntable and sold it to the customer instead. I probably needn't mention that this little solution of his was against the rules. All the money my store had invested in that turntable was lost for at least six weeks. By the time the replacement cover arrived, the turntable had been pilfered into trash as fellow scavengers availed themselves of other hard-to-replace parts.

Multiply such a situation by the number of SKUs you carry, then by your number of employees, and you'll be out of business before you can say "CD." In an age when specialist retailers face competition for their customers' attention from every direction, good management skills are no longer a luxury. We could put up with the Spacemans of the sales force in the "good old days" before Wal-Mart began its march across America and Al Gore invented the Internet. Not so any longer.

You can't let your people decide what's right and what's wrong until you're certain they know the rules. Once they start making decisions based on *your* parameters, you can let them take charge. And when that happy day arrives, you won't worry yourself to death each time you leave the store. You won't have to call every hour to make sure the building is still at the same address. You'll rest well knowing they turned off the air and lights when they closed up.

Unfortunately, not all employees can be motivated to play by your rules. And that's what makes management so difficult. For many folks, one job is as good as another, as long as it pays the rent. The tough part is figuring out who is who before you hire them.

You see, there are two kinds of workers: the willing and the unwilling. The willing may not know their jobs, make regular mistakes, and appear to be from another planet. But they're willing to learn the rules and to change their behavior. The unwilling believe a paycheck is some kind of American right, something they're entitled to in exchange for not being at home. They won't learn because they don't want to. You know these people. You probably employ some now.

When I took over my first store, I inherited a 20-something string bean of a fellow who interpreted every rule as a suggestion. James Zincman wore

> You can't let your people decide what's right and what's wrong until you're certain they know the rules.

torn jeans, rotten sneakers, and an assortment of Harley Davidson T-shirts. In lieu of a traditional 'do, Jimmy opted for what appeared to be some sort of river animal that had taken up residence on his head. He was chronically late, rarely shaved, and seldom attended our Saturday morning sales meetings. My predecessors had pretty much left Jimmy to himself because this attractive fellow was also related to the HR director.

Hiding in my office one day, I was called to the salesfloor to witness a wondrous event: Jimmy had sold $2,000 worth of stereo equipment! Jimmy was as surprised as anyone. He spotted me coming and knew the wide smile on my face was just for him. Ah, the beginning of a beautiful friendship. He grinned, closed his eyes, and spun around, throwing his fist into the sky and shouting, "Yahoo!" As he turned, his fist hit the chin of the woman standing right behind him, knocking her unconscious. And, baby, I mean "lights out!"

The good news was she landed in the arms of her husband, who saved her from the damage of hitting the floor at light speed. He helped her out the door after she quickly came to, and we never heard from them again. (You'd be surprised how often I'm accused of minor exaggeration in my stories. I swear every word of this tale is true. People were just a lot less litigious in those days....)

I really shouldn't have been surprised. I knew Jimmy was a loose cannon my first day as store manager. So, why did I let the situation continue? Claiming my hands were tied because he was the HR director's nephew was simply an excuse. The truth was I had no idea how to control him, or anyone else who worked for me.

Jimmy failed because I failed. And I failed because I had never learned how to manage people. No one had ever taught me that management is more than pushing around paperwork and waiting for disaster to strike. Who knew there are actually rules to follow?! And yet the basic rules are so easy to remember:

RULE #1. Do not sucker punch the customers.

RULE #2. The staff works for you. You do not work for them.

You don't have to be an ogre to be the boss. It *is* possible to create an environment in which employees actually look forward to coming to work. Many of those folks already on your payroll can be trained to clean the store *your* way, stock merchandise, say hello to complete strangers, come in on time, shave once a day, dress properly, and, oh yeah, sell.

Keep turning these pages, and together we'll walk through the steps to such training — as well as methods for conducting effective interviews and employee evaluations… ways to inspire a "specialist attitude" in your staff and keep them ahead of the superstore competition… strategies for giving your people praise, criticism, and a commission plan that will leave them wishing you'd switched your compensation policy years ago…. You know, how to be a great manager!

Before we get into all the nitty-gritty though, I'd like to introduce you to the guys at Sam's Best Brands Plus, some of the many folks at independent retail stores just like yours who you'll meet in the following pages. At Sam's Best Brands Plus, they're already doing things like managing their people by managing their store's data and playing the Show Me Game with their employees — techniques I'll teach you about as we make our way through these pages together.

Read on, and be inspired….

Management is more than pushing around paperwork and waiting for disaster to strike.

Specialist Spotlight on

Sam's Best Brands Plus

One of the longest-running jokes on the television show *The Simpsons* centers on where exactly Homer and Marge's hometown of Springfield is. Springfield, Missouri... Springfield, Massachusetts... perhaps even Springfield, Illinois, home of Sam's Best Brands Plus. Now believe me, the men who own *this* store are no Homers. The Moriconi family, a couple of Sams and a Jeremy, could not only run a nuclear power plant, they could sell it at retail.[1]

Sam Sr. is an articulate man who began as a "shelf stretcher" at Woolco at the age of 18. He proudly recalls that, within a year, he was the youngest appliance manager at any of the company's 250 locations. After taking off some time to try his hand at real estate, Sam joined C.A. Dawson's Furniture & Appliance, and there he truly fell in love... with the people, with retail, and with the success he found as a top-notch salesman. After three years, he graduated to Young's Appliances, a Springfield landmark of more than half a century. Sam felt so at home there that he stayed with Young's for the next 15 years — until the owners decided to close their doors, in fact.

Sam Sr. was facing unemployment, and he wasn't the only one soon to be jobless. Sam Jr. was about to receive his undergraduate degree in business and, like many college grads these days, had few employment prospects. So Sam Jr. said to Sam Sr.: "Why not open our own store?"

Although superstores ranging from Lowe's and Best Buy to Sam's Club and Wal-Mart were springing up all over the cornfields, both father and son had faith in the specialist model. Joining the ranks of the nearest Big Boxes R Us just wasn't for them. They decided to take charge of their careers by taking charge of their own company.

---

[1] Check out their picture on the front cover. That's Sam Sr. in the center with Jeremy on the left and Sam Jr. on the right.

A land developer had torn down the old Fiat-Allis manufacturing plant on Springfield's main drag just outside of town and was putting in a retail center. Not exactly a shopping center — more of a retail neighborhood. Perfect location. The Moriconis bought land, built their store, and opened Sam's Best Brands Plus in September 1997.

They figured their new venture would get off to a slow start. It would take time to get the word out, time they needed to learn a few practical things about running a retail outfit. After all, Sam Sr.'s background was in specialist sales, not store management. They had no such luxury: Customers thronged to Sam's Best Brands Plus even before the official opening, and the place just got fuller and fuller as the week progressed. They'd never seen this kind of business before... anywhere!

Apparently Sam Sr.'s two decades spent earning the community's confidence — his personal trade, as I like to call it — was paying off. His specialist background, product knowledge, and reputation, along with the store's location, were a winning combination.

Sam Sr. was so overwhelmed with the avalanche of customers that he locked his doors. Can you believe that?! He said he needed to catch his breath. It was too difficult to keep an eye on the front door while unloading boxes at the back. Besides, how can you sell products when you haven't organized your paper trail for the receipts? His son flipped out, insisting dad reopen the doors and "figure it all out later."

So Sam Sr. made his first smart management decision: He brought in experienced help. Kelly Pine, the bookkeeper from Young's Appliances, came to the rescue, "slapped my father" back to reality, as Sam Jr. recalls, and got their accounts in order. She was only there a month before handing the reins back to the founding partners. That was then...

> Sam Sr. was so overwhelmed with the avalanche of customers that he locked his doors.

Now, just six years later, Sam Sr.'s other son Jeremy is a partner, and the original staff of five has grown to 28. Sam's Best Brands Plus now has two locations, one selling "dent and scratch" appliances to the discount trade (acquired from manufacturer close-outs) and the other, a 33,000-square-foot beauty, selling top-of-the-line appliances, home theater equipment, carpeting, furniture, and cellular phones. Marge Simpson is in heaven.

Since the three partners are family, they treat everyone who works for them as family, too. Once a month the Moriconis take their entire crew, spouses and children included, out to dinner — not to boost morale or hold an off-site meeting, but simply to say "thanks for your hard work" and to solidify their relationship.

Relations between the owners and the rest of the crew could hardly be stronger: Two of the salespeople came with Sam Sr. from Young's Appliances, and they haven't lost a single employee they've hired in that department since then.

Sam Jr., who acts as both general staff manager and company sales manager, attributes the zero turnover rate among the sales team to the partners' honesty with each other and with their employees. "Never hesitate to confront an uncomfortable situation" is his advice.

When a staff member violates a stated company rule, for example, Sam Jr. calls that employee into his office immediately. He explains why the infraction is detrimental to the store's overall success. He reviews the proper procedure or rule. Then he says: "Do you understand?" If the answer is no, Sam Jr. starts back at the beginning, repeating the process until the employee can repeat in his own words why the rule or procedure is important.

This variation of my Show Me Game (which you'll learn all about in Chapter Five, "The World According to You") is one of the most important tools in the specialist retailer's toolbox. Use it, and you're truly taking charge of your store.

The Moriconis employ another trick of the trade we'll discuss in this book: Always manage your store with the data, because the numbers never, ever lie. Now, Sam Jr. is only 28 years old, and most of his staff members are older, but he doesn't let that intimidate him. The data is the data, and you can't argue with it. There's no whining that Sam Jr. is just a young hotshot throwing his weight around when the sales records or employee evaluation sheets are right there in front of you.

The data can be hard to swallow, though, especially at a small company where you consider everyone family. Some time back, the three partners had a feeling there was a good deal of theft going on in the warehouse. Inventory numbers weren't matching up. As much as you want to believe the people you trust would never cheat you, there's no arguing with such cold, hard facts.

They announced they'd be installing security cameras with continuous video recording throughout the building. And guess what? They caught the thief the very next week. What a Homer! The guy knew the store was under surveillance and stole anyway.

Even the best of families need tough love sometimes. So like all smart retailers, independents and big-box chains alike, the Moriconis prosecute to the max.

They know if they let someone off the hook for whatever reason, they lose all credibility with the rest of their crew. After all, taking charge of

> Like all smart retailers, independents and big-box chains alike, the Moriconis prosecute to the max.

your store means *staying* in charge when things get rough, regardless of how uncomfortable the situation.

Ah, Springfield… The name itself conjures up a feeling of simplicity and days gone by. With a market base of 100,000 people, however, it's hardly quaint. But it is, I'm told, a good place to bring up children. Sam Sr. did such a good job the first time, he's going for round two. He and his new wife are expecting their first child together. Perhaps I should mention Sam Jr. and his new wife are expecting their first child, as well. With Lisa, Bart, and Maggie in town, they'll be in good company.

Chapter 2
Just the Facts, Ma'am

So, weary managers, we learned in Chapter One that there's plenty of good news about retailing today. It *is* possible to assemble a team of responsible human beings who do what you want them to do! Not because you said so, but because it needs to be done. All you, their supreme leader, need is a little direction, instruction, and encouragement. (And, sometimes, a stretcher.) Now let's turn our attention to the very important difference between *things* and *people*.

Things are much easier to manage than people. Things stay at work overnight and are there bright and early in the morning. Things don't have an attitude. They never argue, lie, steal, or sucker punch the customers. Things will do whatever you tell them to do. They recognize that you're the boss, *el jefe*, the big cheese.

As retail managers, our lists of things screaming for attention seem endless: reports for the main office, computer registers on the blink, overstock, and understaffing. But the most important things the effective retail manager deals with are numbers, all kinds of them. Numbers tell you precisely what is going on in your store.

Looking at a profit-and-loss statement or balance sheet is about as enjoyable as going to the dentist. These things are black and white and boring all over. When I try to have a little fun and get creative with my reports, it looks like I'm embezzling. Unfortunately, like regular dental cleanings, P&Ls and balance sheets are a necessary evil — but they are also just as easy to put off. In fact, let's do that right now.... You'll find some great resources in Appendix A for taking charge of your financial statements.

We're going to concentrate in *this* book on something a lot more enjoyable than how to assemble reports that would make your accountant proud: the good news that by managing *things* — like sales data or inventory turns — your attempts to manage *people* suddenly become much easier. The data about your store will tell you what decisions to make about your people. Why is this, you ask? Because the data never, ever lies.

I learned this lesson when I worked for Simone Lagree. This woman was rude, mean, and unattractive. She also owned the company. It must have been my first week there when I strolled into her office, a mistake I quickly learned not to repeat. I told her I was working on the solution to a problem and needed "two or three things" from her.

At the top of her lungs, the woman shrieked like a she-dragon with a bullhorn: "Is the number two or three?! Are these numbers *too big* for you to keep track of? There is a 50% difference between those two numbers! If you can't count to three, how are you going to handle real numbers?! Get out of my office!"

I think I actually limped from the room. My co-workers just laughed. "Don't ever go into that office unless you have every detail of every fact," they said. They were actually surprised she was as "nice" to me as she was. I guess it's because I was the new guy.

In the future, I stayed away from this woman at all costs. On the few occasions I had to see her in the course of my duties, I carried more data than the Starship *Enterprise*. And darned if it didn't turn out that many times after collecting all that data, the solution to my problem was obvious. Although she was an unforgiving banshee, she taught me a great lesson: The data has the answers.

Consider your store's utilities, one of my favorite examples of easily managed things. If your electric bill quadruples overnight, you know you have a problem. Have you been working late on the books recently, with the entire store lit up like a landing field? Has someone reset the air conditioning so it's on all night keeping the mice comfortable? Something or someone has increased your utility bill. It's a fact right there on the monthly statement in front of you. Now you have a good reason to spend precious time tracking down the someone or something responsible.

You should manage your employees with such facts, as well.

Jill hasn't sold enough to buy your parakeet lunch. She can argue all she wants to, give you an Academy Award-winning excuse, and levitate around the room like that flying nun. None of these feats will change the numbers on the report in front of you. The truth remains: Jill is not pulling her weight. What are you going to do about it?

When dealing with your staff, remember that they're human beings, too. And human beings have a tendency to remember things differently from the facts.

Consider my own situation. If, on a rare occasion, I perform some marital infraction, my wife seems to think I do it "all the time." I'd only have to remember a single incident when I didn't do whatever I've been accused of doing and I'd be able to present a decent defense. Now, I *could* keep a logbook of things I do and don't do "all the time" to prove my wife's error. Such data would be valuable evidence if I planned to live alone for the rest of my life.

It's different at work, though. At work, you're attempting to correct behavior in order to increase profits. At work, a misconception can cost you thousands of dollars. At home, only your marriage.

> When dealing with your staff, remember that they're human beings, too.

When I worked as the sales director for an electronics firm, one of my salesmen wanted to give away $300-worth of company-branded T-shirts to one of his accounts. The store was having a promotional event and wanted to advertise free T-shirts as an incentive to bring customers in. His idea made sense. This was exactly the kind of event for which we'd bought the T-shirts.

I had just one small question: How much business (in cold, hard U.S. dollars) does this customer do with us? I simply wanted him to justify the expense. Apparently, it had never dawned on my people that our shirts cost money. They seemed to think the T-shirt fairy dropped them from the sky pre-printed with our logo.

My salesguy pleaded with me: The store owner was a "great customer" and deserved our support. I told him to get out his spreadsheet for the last 12 months, and we'd see how "great" the customer was. Well, based on the data, that $300 in T-shirts represented 24% of the dealer's total annual purchases. You can't give a customer back a quarter of the money he gave you!

"Oh, we're not giving him *money*," my guy replied innocently. "We're giving him T-shirts."

I explained that, according to the data, the dealer had a sleeve and wash tag coming to him at no charge.

"Oh, come on!" he said. "He's a real nice guy and a loyal dealer."

"Then tell me you want to support him because he's a nice guy," I replied. "That makes more sense to me than trying to get free goods based on the assertion that he's a great dealer."

I ended up giving him 10 shirts, not 30. At the end of the promotion, all of that store's employees were wearing nice, new, crisp, clean, logo-branded T-shirts. They got them from their sales rep. From the staff's point of view, their rep was a "great salesman."

Because I leaned on the data so hard, I was famous within that company for not giving away free T-shirts — or $10 bills.

The data will save you a ton of money. I used to hate the V.P. of finance for giving me orders from the corporate office when I was a store manager. "Hey!" I thought to myself. "If you want to run this store, come down here and do it yourself!" But I'll be dipped if he wasn't right 75% of the time. It kills me to say it today, but I was wrong. (Of course, I'll never admit this in writing.)

The other 25% of the time is just as critical, however. You must gather your intelligence on the salesfloor, too. You can't rely on spreadsheets alone; although without them, you won't even know where to begin.

The same thing is true with your staff. The data can tell you all kinds of things that may slip through the cracks: things like how often they're late for work or out sick, how many grandparents they've had die....

And the beauty of the data is that no one can argue with it. Start managing these things, and you'll have a much easier time managing your people — a theme you'll hear throughout these pages. For now, let's see how the manager of Gotta Go Wireless uses data to keep his store operating as smoothly as a cell phone on a wide open stretch of highway.

The beauty of the data is that no one can argue with it.

Specialist Spotlight on

Gotta Go Wireless

"Data tells me everything!" boasts Andy Wirth, owner of the Gotta Go Wireless store on Oracle Road in Tucson, Arizona. Perhaps it's all those zeros and ones used in digital transmissions, but Andy is just a numbers kind of guy.

Andy was working as a sales manager for Cellular One back in the late 1990s, with as many as 20 reps reporting to him, when disillusionment about corporate life started setting in. Sure, the company's management was good, and the money was great… but the job came with too much stress. He didn't feel as if he had enough control over certain important elements of his job — offering personal attention to customers, for example. This lack of control was translating to an unhappiness with his overall quality of life. Besides, the kids at home were growing up way too fast.

Bottom line: Andy wanted to take charge of his career so he could stay in charge of his life. Sound familiar?

About that time, a friend came up with the concept for a specialist wireless store called Gotta Go Wireless. Andy liked the name — and the financial potential — of the store so much that he talked his buddy into letting him license the name. In May 2000, Andy officially joined the ranks of independent specialist retailers when his own 1,200-square-foot Gotta Go Wireless store opened. "I'm really glad I made the change," he says. "I used to work 13, 14 hours at the office, and still be taking phone calls from my people at home after that. Now, when I'm home, I'm home."

Tracking data at Gotta Go Wireless involves four — yes, *four* — separate systems. First, Andy maintains a file with hard copies of all paperwork for each of his clients. Service applications, original receipts, whatever…

You could call Andy up in the middle of a desert thunderstorm with all the electricity out and he'd still be able to pull up your information.

Second, he keeps an up-to-the-minute Excel spreadsheet to track all detailed customer information: phone model, service plan, contract expiration date, add-on services, and on and on. "This may sound hokey, but the Excel spreadsheet is working well," he says. It should. He's spent three years fine-tuning it to perfectly fit his, and his clients' needs, after all.

Andy prints out these spreadsheets for review every single day, then places follow-up phone calls to his clients. The personal touch obviously works: Repeat customers account for 75% of the business at Gotta Go Wireless. The word-of-mouth advertising that Andy enjoys from these happy clients is so positive that potential clients, walking into Gotta Go Wireless, will actually wait — quite happily! — for 20 minutes or more until Andy or his sales assistant finish with the previous customer.

The third tracking system at Gotta Go Wireless is a commissions report for the cellular carriers, so that the service providers know exactly how much to pay Andy for selling their products. Talk about a proactive approach to business! There's no sitting around just waiting for the payment checks to wander on in at Gotta Go Wireless.

The store's fourth data-tracking program is a web-based system that allows Andy to upload information on how many activations the store sold for which carrier. "I update these reports weekly," Andy says.

His background as a sales manager is probably a major influence on his understanding of how much you can do with the data to increase your

> The personal touch obviously works: Repeat customers account for 75% of the business at Gotta Go Wireless.

business. "When I was a sales manager, tracking employees' performance was crucial," he says. "Now, the data helps me recognize the potential for more business. If you don't keep track of whatever numbers are pertinent to your store or industry, you will affect your bottom line. Still, I don't think I track as much as I could." What a modest guy.

If all independent specialists tracked their data in four completely separate ways — and then made daily follow-up phone calls to their customers — Wal-Mart would be out of business.

You needn't be as thorough as Andy is to be an effective manager. Yet there's no doubt that, the more data you have, the better your ability to take charge of your store. Look at data the way you look at your car's speedometer: You don't absolutely need it to operate the vehicle, but it sure makes for a safer drive.

Chapter 3
To Commission or Not to Commission

Managing your people by keeping regular tabs on things like sales data and overhead expenses only gets you halfway towards your goal of taking charge of your store. The category of *things* known as your compensation program is so important we're now going to devote an entire chapter to it.

I believe in paying people for the amount of work they do. If Mary does a lot, she should be paid a lot. If her performance is, eh, so-so, her paycheck should reflect that. If she's not contributing to your store's success, she should be taught how. And if she has no desire to learn, she should be fired.

Sound too harsh? Ah, you're suffering from that ailment typical among managers, the Misplaced Manners Syndrome — just as I did before Jimmy of the flailing limbs caused an incident that today would have lawyers lining up outside my store with visions of settlements dancing in their heads.

Even for many of us in the retail industry, commissioned salespeople are about as well regarded as the stereotypical used-car (excuse me, pre-owned vehicle) salesman. They're pushy, rude, and care only about making a buck, right? No! You could say the Pushy Salesman is the U.S. retail equivalent of Europe's Ugly American Traveler — you know, the gum-snapping, videocam-toting tourists who seem to think that if they only speak English loudly enough, the natives will understand them.

You can't blame Europeans for getting the impression that all Americans are like this. Who's going to notice the couple from Normal, Illinois, quietly asking directions of a vendor in St. Mark's Square when

Bertha's over the way arguing with the entrance guard about wearing shorts into *Il Domo*?

The point is: *If* your commissioned salespeople are good enough at their jobs, your customers won't ever realize they are on commission.

When you operate on commission, though, you have to expect your best people to make some pretty good money — perhaps even more than you. A friend who used to work in the camera business told me about working with a terrific salesman who made so much money on commission... he got fired. He was offered a management position at a flat salary and he turned it down, so they let him go. Can you imagine that? Some upper-management knucklehead saw this guy making more money than he was and couldn't stand it.

The bottom line is: The more money your star salespeople are making for themselves, *the more money they're making for your company.* How can that possibly be bad news?!

Compare the above story with that of my friend, co-owner of a $100-million-a-year corporation, whose salary is less than half that of his partner. I once asked him why one makes so much more than the other if they're partners. He responded without a trace of resentment: "I'm the operations manager. My partner actually generates income for the corporation. He's worth more, therefore he makes more."

Whether you sell books or bicycles, your goal is to have the highest paid sales staff in your industry. That's taking charge of your store!

So, how do we get to that point? Managers face two major hurdles when instituting a commission program: figuring out how to set up the program, and then figuring out how to sell your employees on it. The good news is that a carefully planned commission program will sell itself to your people. You just have to know how to go about it.

Many people shy away from commission-based jobs. Maybe they've never been taught real sales skills. Maybe they're just uncomfortable about their own abilities. Whatever the reason, these folks are afraid they won't be able to make it and feel more comfortable with a guaranteed wage.

I know exactly how they feel. I was scared to death when I first started in retail. I'd worked as a professional musician since college. Then I woke up one day to find myself 34 years old and in need of something a little steadier than "nightclub entertainer" to take care of my child, car payments, and apartment. "Just show up, and you'll sell enough to pay the rent," said the manager of the stereo shop that hired me.

Showing up for my first day of what we entertainers called "civilian life" was easy. It was what followed that terrified me about life in the retail world. Although the store opened at 9:00 a.m., at five minutes after the hour the cashier and I were still huddled by the back door trying to stay dry in the pelting rain. Things did not improve from there.

I mistook my boss for a hippie biker/serial killer when he finally showed up at the flooded building with the keys. Perhaps it was the waist-length hair and conspicuous absence of shoes. I spent the rest of the day aghast, water vacuum in hand, watching my new colleagues stand ankle-deep in the wet stuff while playing with live amplifiers. It was an electrifying start to my specialist sales career.

I eventually discovered that this crew included some of the best salespeople I'd ever have the privilege of working with, personal appear-

> I mistook my boss for a hippie biker/ serial killer when he finally showed up at the flooded building.

ances and notions of water safety aside. In the good old days before hi-fi shops became "home theater specialists," you could get away with stuff like that — *if* you knew your merchandise and you knew how to sell it. And sell they did.

The sink-or-swim (literally, in my case) method of learning how to do commissioned sales is hardly how you want to present your program to prospective employees. But, tell those applicants that you're going to show them *how* to do their jobs and, thereby, help them succeed, and they'll be a lot less intimidated about joining your team.

Add to that the good news that your employees can give themselves raises any old time they want to. They just have to sell more. We'll go into more detail at the end of this chapter about selling your current team on commissions, if you now pay hourly.

First, though, let's review some basics of commission structure, starting with the fact that commission is based on either gross profit or gross sales (often called just "gross").

Paying on gross profit — which means your salespeople receive a percentage of the profit made on each deal — is essential if you allow your people to discount merchandise. If you don't pay on gross profit and allow your people to negotiate with customers, they'll sell everything at cost — making a fortune for themselves and nothing for you. If you do pay on gross profit, your people are discounting their own paychecks if they discount the merchandise.

About half of the specialist music retailers I've met allow their employees to negotiate prices with the customers, as do many independent retailers in the mobile and consumer electronics markets.

Gross profit is a product's selling price minus its cost. So, if a mountain bike helmet costs you $60, and you sell it for $100, your gross profit is $40. Your salesperson would receive a percentage of the $40. That percentage can be as little as 15% and as high as 22%. (As with any incentive program, you should always leave room to grow.)

When I worked the salesfloor, my commission began at 17% of the gross profit. If I reached a certain volume level — at a particular margin (a reward for not giving products away) — that percentage would rise a point or two. I didn't just make commission on the goods I sold, I got a bonus point or two for selling a large amount at higher margins. By selling more, I made more. That's always good news!

Paying on gross sales — which means that your salespeople receive a percentage of the sales ticket — is the way to go if your prices are non-negotiable. Using the example of the mountain bike helmet, if you pay on gross sales, your employee would receive a percentage of the $100 sales ticket for that item.

You can see that commission percentages for paying on gross sales are necessarily much smaller — in the low single-digits — than the 15% or more that salespeople would receive under a gross-profit plan.

Straightforward plans based on either gross profit or gross sales aren't your only two choices when you decide to go the commission route. Retailers can also add a little spice to basic plans with a few "spiffs."

A spiff refers to an item's "specific bonus." In other words, offer a bounty on certain items. This is especially helpful in moving merchandise that's been around so long it should be paying rent. Offer your staff $5 in addition to their normal commission to sell it. It won't be there long.

> Straightforward plans based on either gross profit or gross sales aren't your only two choices.

Retailers sometimes make the mistake of having items "spiffed" for too long, however. You might, for example, spiff an expensive camera because it has a lot of profit in it. Even with the spiff, it's the most profitable camera you carry. After a year or so, the camera is selling so well you decide to drop the incentive. But you've been spiffing the camera for so long your crew interprets this change as a cut in wages, and they stop selling the camera altogether.

Used wisely, a spiff program can move a lot of dead merchandise. Remember, inventory is like putting money in a no-interest bank account. It's worth less everyday. So spiff wisely and spiff often!

Once you start thinking about how to give your sales team financial incentives to sell, there's no limit to the kinds of creative programs specialist retailers can put in place. For example, try paying hourly and put a different spiff on the more profitable, harder-to-sell items. If an employee wants a raise, he can try selling those more challenging items. It costs you nothing, because you already make more money on those selected items. That's precisely why you can afford to pay a higher commission on them.

Of course, it's possible for this system to backfire on you — and that's the source of everyone's fear when it comes to buying from a commissioned salesperson, isn't it? There's always the salesperson who intentionally sells the wrong item to someone just to make more money.

The good news is that this scenario truly is the exception rather than the rule. A professional and honest employee knows that filling a customer's needs, rather than his own pocket, will make him far more money in the long run. Self-serving employees don't last long, regardless of their position. Please don't let that "what if" scenario keep you from going after your goal: getting your money's worth out of every member of your sales team.

Even if you're blessed with a dynamite sales staff, the news that you're planning to switch to a commission-pay basis will threaten them. Some will want to bail immediately. They're so used to a guaranteed paycheck that they won't settle for less. But there *is* a way to make the transition so that it does not intimidate anyone.

STEP #1: Start accepting applications. Post a sign that reads "Now Accepting Applications" where everyone can see it. (Just make sure you don't use one that implies you are actually *looking* to hire someone. You'll open yourself to all kinds of accusations from applicants who claim you didn't hire them for reasons of discrimination.)

What you want are some living bodies lined up in case your current staff decides to leave you on the spot. You can't put off implementing your exciting new incentive-pay program just because you're afraid of being left shorthanded.

STEP #2: Determine who is selling what. A point-of-sale computer program that assigns each person a sales identification number is the easiest way to do this. The POS application should provide reports both on total sale amounts and individual items on each invoice. Then you can see each employee's total sales figures, as well as what merchandise is making up those sales. Monitoring the reports for two or three months will give you an accurate picture of your sales trends.

What your people sell is very important. Some salespeople don't sell certain items because they don't believe in the merchandise. When I was a sales manager for an independent electronics specialist, I found

> You can't put off implementing your exciting new incentive-pay program just because you're afraid of being left shorthanded.

out from one of these POS reports that one of my best salesguys didn't sell any car alarms. None! When questioned, he told me he didn't believe in them. I explained he didn't need to believe in them, he just needed to sell them. He thought that was unethical. So, I sat him down and sold *him* on the benefits of mobile security. His sales in that category picked up.

Salespeople will also avoid certain products or categories because they have limited information or understanding about them. Say an employee in a cycling shop never attempts to sell crank sets with hollowtech design as add-ons to bike purchases. She has probably never had anyone explain to her in plain English the practical benefits of this fancier gear technology — so, of course, she can't explain the value, much less the purpose, of such a profitable add-on item to anyone else.

Whatever their reasons, you can't let your employees pick and choose what they want to sell.

One tip: Whether you're installing a new POS system or just reviewing procedure on the old one, do not tell your crew that this is the beginning of a new era in pay scales! They'll spend the whole first day worrying about finding another job.

STEP #3: Get out the calculator. We'll assume that you are paying on gross sales, not gross profit. With reports in hand, look at each employee's average monthly sales. Then calculate what percentage of the gross is equal to the amount you currently pay that person.

For example, you pay Frank $10 an hour, which, at 40 hours a week, comes out to $1,600 a month. Your POS report says that Frank's average monthly gross is $11,000. After playing with your calculator for a few minutes, you'll find that if you pay Frank $8 an hour base wage ($1,280) plus a 3% commission ($330), he'll collect $1,610. That's $10 *above* his monthly "draw," or what he would be making at his regular hourly rate.

Depending on your situation, you'll have to play with the base salary and percentage figure to make it come out "right." What you're trying to do, of course, is demonstrate to Frank that, under a commission-based plan, if he sells exactly what he sells now, , he can take home at least the equivalent of his current paycheck.

STEP #4: Share the good news with your staff. Once you've gotten your data ready, gather your people and announce that the store will be switching to a commission program. Cut short their fears by telling them straight off: "The good news is that if you just do what you're doing now, you'll bring home the same amount of money."

But the gooder news is: "If you increase your output — and I'm going to teach you how — you have the opportunity to make a really good living." Then show them a sample POS and talk to them about where they're missing sales opportunities. Allow three to four minutes for whining and sniveling. Then get everyone back to work!

> If you just do what you're doing now, you'll bring home the same amount of money.

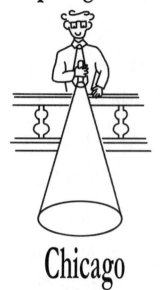

Specialist Spotlight on

Chicago Brass

Decorative Plumbing and Hardware

Chicago Brass... The name sounds more like a big band than a hardware store. But when you speak with owner C.J. Schnakenberg, you can see why he doesn't mind blowing his own horn. Hardware is in his blood.

In the 1920s, C.J.'s grandfather and great-grandfather opened a hardware store to serve the many factories on the Windy City's north side: Ace Hardware Store No. 8, to be exact. Not surprisingly, C.J.'s own father ended up working in the store, raising a family as well as a customer base.

Yes, indeed, C.J. Schnakenberg was born with a silver hinge in his mouth. He still laughs heartily when reminiscing about childhood exploits at the store…. Like the time a very unhappy dad caught him and his two older siblings merrily throwing glazing putty at each other in the aisles.

Like many kids though, C.J. didn't want to go into the family business. He wanted something "better," something more exciting than hardware. So he went to college and graduated in 1976 with a degree in political science. Talk about exciting! But a poli sci degree doesn't lead to too many obvious career choices… so C.J. ended up joining the family business, after all.

As he settled in at Ace Hardware Store No. 8 and learned to love the work, C.J. began noticing a change in the products customers were looking for. Requests for hammers and nails were giving way to queries about special-order items like mortise locks and custom hardware sets.

By the mid-1980s, such requests were so frequent that C.J. saw his chance to specialize. In 1985, he opened up Chicago Brass Decorative Plumbing and Hardware to serve the wealthy North Shore area.

Just as his forefathers founded their hardware store to cater to local factory managers, rather than simply to offer general hardware supplies, C.J. chose a very specific target customer: the contractors and interior designers working on the North Shore's pricey homes. To appeal to them, he would offer just the really good stuff — items like $1,000 lock sets for $5 million mansions.

Of course, the weekend do-it-yourselfer finds as warm a welcome from the Chicago Brass staff as anyone else. C.J. just doesn't go out of his way to draw them away from Great Indoors and Home Depot Expo, his area's two big-box competitors.

Although the majority of his business is with the building trade, many of his walk-in customers are the homeowners themselves. In some cases, their contractors have sent them over to look at options for their construction or renovation projects. In others, the homeowners took the initiative and plan to send their contractors in later. And on occasion, customers tell the Chicago Brass team that "someone at Home Depot sent me over here." Praise indeed!

With a client base that combines hard-working contractors and wealthy homeowners, C.J.'s employees certainly need to be specialists — not just in current trends and technical requirements for new-home construction, but in how to deal tactfully with a variety of people. It's not good news if potential customers hear the *ka-ching* of dollar signs in your employees' eyes when they walk through your doors.

Happily, some of C.J.'s core staff of 10 or so had come with him from the family store when he founded Chicago Brass. Among the veteran team members is his store manager, with whom C.J. has now worked for more than 20 years.

> Customers tell the Chicago Brass team that "someone at Home Depot sent me over."

"Succeeding as a specialist retailer is all about caring for the customer," C.J. says. "The big-box guys want the sale today. They push for it. At Chicago Brass, we know that when a customer is spending tens of thousands of dollars on hardware sets, it may take months for the sale to go down. That's why we don't need to push — but rather nurture — our customers."

Sounds like this high-end specialist store would be the last place to operate on commission, doesn't it? Yet C.J. knew early on that adopting an incentive-based pay structure was the only way to run the store.

The first time he instituted a commission program, however, stealing each other's customers and selling only those products they personally made more money on seemed to be the order of the day. Customers were suddenly rich folks to gouge as quickly as possible.

Nothing could have been more opposite to C.J.'s philosophy that rich people have special needs... including the need to do business with salespeople who can see past their money and become just as excited about their home projects as they are.

So, C.J. kept at it until he found a way to make his commission-based plan work, going through a fair amount of turnover in the process. The secret, it seems, is not so much how you *structure* a commission-based program, but how you *oversee* it. C.J. knows that it's not the commission program that makes salespeople shady — it's the individual salesperson.

So both he and his manager work the floor, keeping a close eye to ensure that everyone is working within the bounds of their store's culture. And as long as the two of them stay involved in the workings of the store, the commission program works great.

Being knowledgeable and passionate about the special products Chicago Brass carries is just half the equation, however.

"You see, it's not how we do sales that makes us special. It's why we do it," C.J. says. And they do it for all the right reasons: People are great, and business is fun.

Yet having fun on the job is more than just about making work enjoyable. It can be integral to making the sale — a notion C.J. works hard to instill in his employees. Just the other day, a contractor sent a client into Chicago Brass to look at several special items. A salesperson approached the woman and asked if she had any questions. "Just looking" came the reply.

So C.J. approached the woman and explained in mock-confidential tones that the poor salesguy had an extremely fragile ego. If she didn't ask him a question, he'd feel rejected and would take a day or two to recover. The lady laughed and admitted she did have some questions after all.

"It's all about relationships," C.J. says. "Most of these people have servants and employees taking care of everything in their lives. They want someone they can talk to, one on one, without feeling placated. They want to feel comfortable." With most of C.J.'s new customers coming through word-of-mouth advertising, he and his team must be making their current clients comfortable indeed.

The original family hardware store closed in 2000 after the rent on their space tripled, but C.J.'s own children are keeping up the family tradition by working in Chicago Brass part time. He's not sure any of them are going to make it a living, though. His oldest, studying to be a first class

> Having fun on the job is more than just about making work enjoyable.

sailor, just received his First Mate papers. Dad's proud of him, of course. As for the younger kids... who knows. Even if his eldest doesn't decide to lead the way for the fifth generation to enter the family business, however, C.J. and his team of hardware specialists will have no trouble keeping Chicago Brass afloat.

I don't think I've ever held a management position where I didn't have to fire my top salesperson at some point. In many cases, your "star employees" are not actually making you money. In fact, they could be costing you big time. Think about it.... These guys rarely lend a hand with the chores, they show up for work when they want, and they rack up a ton of sales. As a result, the rest of your people (and not just the sales team) resent them. Such hard feelings create a hostile atmosphere that affects your customers — and ultimately your bottom line.

Consider the 17-store retail chain I once did a product seminar for during my manufacturer's rep days. I knew it was going to be a bad day when the company's "top" salesguys showed up drunk for the mid-week seminar. One of the $60K-a-year employees was even clutching a beer can. Their behavior was so disruptive I ended the meeting 15 minutes into my presentation, packed up my materials, and left.

The next day the owner telephoned, embarrassed and apologetic: "Those guys are a pain, but I'm not going to fire them. It was their day off. And besides, they make me too much money." I gave him my "They're Actually Costing You Money" speech and then shut up. I'd been brought in to do a product seminar, not management consulting. We rescheduled for the following month.

By the time I returned, both guys had quit. And guess what? The company was still in business, and the sales numbers for the two stores they worked at hadn't changed a bit. Seems their co-workers had picked up the slack, and morale was sky high.

Are *your* employees holding you hostage? If you can honestly answer, "No, I'd just like to learn how to get the best possible performance

Chapter 4
Assembling Your Specialist Team

from my people," fabulous! This chapter is not for you. Skip ahead to the Spotlight on Page 52 for a little inspiration and then dive right into Chapter Five.

But, if you wouldn't even describe your current employees as diamonds in the rough, let's get working.

I suggested earlier that you post a "Now Accepting Applications" sign as part of your commission plan strategy. I'll repeat that suggestion here, because it is so important. Hang the sign where everyone can see it — *and don't take it down*. Ever. And *do not* use one that says, "Now Hiring." You are not hiring. You're simply announcing that you're always interested in meeting people who would like to work for your store.

The first day you post the sign, your employees will ask if you're looking to make a change. Tell them, "We'll see" — and you'll never again have to put up with the kind of baloney some people insist is their right in return for a paycheck. Over the next few weeks, you'll meet some of the nicest, most willing applicants you could ever imagine. Collect their resumes and application forms. Start telephoning the best of the bunch when you've gotten the guts to fire those folks holding you hostage and set up some interviews.

A word about resumes before we get to the actual interviews.

Having read way too many that would qualify for the Pulitzer Prize in fiction, I seldom take resumes seriously. Especially when it comes to sales — most of the applicants you meet will say they were the "top" performer at their last job. In fact, many were so successful they don't work there anymore. Take the time to follow up. Call an applicant's most recent employer and find out (if you can) if he was indeed the worker he is representing himself to be. For the most part, HR departments will only say whether or not they would hire the candidate back. Thank goodness not all of them are that professional.

After your intelligence gathering, it's time for the actual interviews. Here are a few pointers for getting the most out of those meetings:

TIP #1. Watch body language carefully.

When you ask a candidate into your office, the first thing you should look for is attitude. How does he sit in the chair? Leaning forward or on the edge of the seat? If so, he's eager and interested. Someone lounging back with legs crossed wouldn't be my first choice. I want people who are at least smart enough to try to fool me. Convince me you're dying to work for me! Project an attitude that says something more than, "I need a job."

TIP #2. Realize that sometimes it's okay to judge by appearances.

Is the applicant dressed to impress? I don't care if the job is for a stockroom slave. Quality employees know the difference between dressing for the interview and dressing for the first day of work. If the person is so young he obviously doesn't know any better — *and* you like him — send him home to change. If he returns, you've taught him two things: how to dress for an interview, and that you're a manager of conviction. You've also learned a few important things about him: He really wants the job, and he's got his pride under control. Two great signs.

A salesman who worked for a competitor called me one day when I was working as vice president for a large regional specialist. Things were so bad at the other store he just had to leave. He asked if I had any open-

> I want people who are at least smart enough to try to fool me.

ings, and I invited him in for an interview that very afternoon. He said he'd come straight from work when his shift ended in a few hours.

My jaw dropped when he walked in. A flamboyant mustard stain decorated his shirt. A spot on his pants grew some kind of science project. Before I could stop myself, I blurted out, "Did you go to work dressed like that?!" Puzzled, he replied that he had. "Go home and change, come back, and I'll interview you," I said, adding that the way he was dressed was no way to come to an interview, let alone show up for work.

He phoned soon after. He said he'd been thinking things over and had decided to sue my company for discrimination. I told him to go fly a kite. Fifteen minutes after that he called my sales manager and asked if he could interview with him, instead. He'd just threatened the vice president of the company with a lawsuit and still thought we'd hire him!

Over the years, I've sent many applicants home to change their clothes. Most were just inexperienced and hadn't had anyone — mentor, parent, friend — to teach them otherwise. Most of them returned. And for the most part, I hired those who did.

I have one very important caveat with regard to this advice. Do not send someone home to change out of soiled clothing if his attire is religious, ethnic, or in any way suggests something about the applicant that you may not use as a criteria for employment, because the law views it as discriminatory (Tip #5 discusses the criteria you may not use in hiring decisions).

TIP #3. Tailor your questions to get information you REALLY want.

When you sit down with an applicant, don't wing it. Be prepared with questions designed to gather the kind of information you really need, such as how on-the-ball, motivated, honest, et cetera the applicant is. The following queries have always worked well for me:

Give me a two-minute review of the last movie you saw or book you read. I'm not looking for something to do Saturday night. I just want to see how well the applicant speaks. Does she paint pictures with language, or does she struggle to put three words together in a row? A salesperson who cannot communicate enthusiasm and excitement about your merchandise should not be on your salesfloor.

How much money would you like to make? My philosophy is, "The more unrealistic, the better!" I want someone who will go for it, especially when I'm talking about my sales team, not just someone who's looking for work.

And if the person has been in sales for years and has nothing to show for it — no nice home, no kids in college, not even a hospital wing in his name — he needs to work for the competition. I can't afford him.

As a rule, if a candidate seems uncomfortable with the great incentive-pay program you put together after reading Chapter Three, it means he wants a guaranteed paycheck whether he earns it or not. And if you find someone who's happy with minimum wage, you know you've got the wrong person.

To be fair, let's keep in mind that most applicants have probably only worked on commission at stores where managers do not provide the kind of fantastic on-the-job training and support you'll offer after reading this book. If you've got a good feeling about an applicant, take an extra five minutes during the interview to walk her through the benefits of both your commission plan and your sales training program.

> If you find someone who's happy with minimum wage, you know you've got the wrong person.

Where would you like to be in five years? The further down the line the better. Some good answers: "I want your job." "I want to own my own business." "I'd like to be in a position where I can go back to school."

Some questionable answers: "I want to take my band on tour" (every musician I ever hired left me without notice), or "I want to be a golf pro" ("Hey, it's a beautiful day and that new guy isn't here...."). The common denominator in such answers is that, more than likely, these people have another job besides the one you are hiring them for. Odds are they won't be reliable team members because their loyalties lie some-place between you and the 18th hole.

Is there anything not in this application you would like to discuss before you leave? You'll get answers to this question that will blow your socks off. "Well, since you asked, I have a five-week trip in two months that's planned and paid for." "Yes, I often cross-dress under my street clothes." If the two of you wear the same size, that might be okay.

What questions do you have for me? After interviewing a candidate, ask if he'd like to interview you. Surely he must want to know something about your company: wages, vacation policy, medical coverage, and so on. An applicant who has no questions is probably desperate for a job. You need people who want to work for *your* store, not just *any* store.

TIP #4. Let the applicant do the talking.

How often have you interviewed people who were so enamored with themselves, they didn't let you talk? Well, guess what... This is okay!

You can't learn anything about a prospective team member while you're doing the talking. Ask your questions and then sit back and listen.

Without coming right out and saying so, you're looking to discern the applicant's level of responsibility, work ethic, and ability to grasp new ideas and situations quickly. It would be nice if the person already knew how to do the job, but that's really not so important. You're going to retrain most of the people you hire, anyway.

Long answers allow you to determine an applicant's articulateness, perhaps the most essential skill for a salesperson in specialist retailing. You can teach people how to sell. You can't teach them how to communicate.

I once interviewed a man with a foreign accent so thick I thought English was his third language. It was actually his fifth. This guy painted such vivid pictures in my head with his words that I *had* to put him on the salesfloor. I've also worked with college-educated, native-born Americans who could barely pronounce their own addresses. That's why you want to get people talking.

TIP #5. Learn how to avoid legal minefields.

A woman arrives at your office for a job interview. You notice she's wearing an engagement ring, but no wedding band, or is obviously eight and three-quarters months pregnant with twins. You do what any of us (well, my female readers, at least) would do: Say something friendly like "Are you recently engaged? How exciting!" or "When is the due date?" This is just normal, polite behavior among civilized adults, right? *Wrong!* If you don't hire this woman, and she decides you made the decision based on her (pending) marital or parental status, you will likely find yourself at the losing end of a discrimination lawsuit.

Whether an applicant is married or has children are by no means the only criteria by which you may *not* judge the person's suitability for

> You can teach people how to sell. You can't teach them how to communicate.

employment. The interviewer's oh-so-simple task these days is to avoid asking *any* question, even in casual conversation, that may elicit *any* of the following information about the applicant: race, religion, color, sex, age, national origin, ancestry, marital status (including whether someone is pregnant or has children), physical or mental disability, veteran status, and sexual orientation.

And those aren't the only legal minefields either. One of my favorite interview questions used to be, "Describe the house you grew up in." (Not that I cared; I was trying to determine how articulate the applicant was.) Alas, this question is not such a good idea anymore. Why in the world not?! The interviewer could possibly glean from the answer certain information about the applicant's socio-economic status or background. What was it that Shakespeare said about all the lawyers...?

TIP #6. Beware the "pre-trained" employee.

Just because someone has worked in retail before does not mean he knows anything about it. "Hey, I've worked for everybody in town, and now it's your turn." A short-handed manager can allow her desperate situation to color her better judgment. You'll be training every new employee how to do specialist retailing your way anyway, so you might as well find the best material to work with, regardless of "experience."

TIP #7. Remember you can't afford NOT to pick and choose.

If you want to stand out from the Wal-Marts, you must employ the right people. It's okay *not* to like anyone in your initial round of interviews. You don't have that many staff positions, so hold out for the best workers you can find. A superstore can afford to compromise. Mediocre employees will get lost in the shuffle — and besides, no one shops at a superstore for service anyway, right? But one mediocre person on your team can do a great deal of damage to your image. Prices aside, the main difference between one store and another is the people who work there.

Congratulations! You've just finished Eddy Kay's Crash Course in Hiring a Darn Good Retail Team.

Of course, I haven't told you anything here you couldn't learn from the management column in one of your industry trade magazines — and, if you ever had time to finish those magazine articles piled on your desk, you'd know that! But what retail manager has time to read? Well, you will — now that you'll be cutting down on your employee turnover by hiring the right people the first time around.

Besides, if you're holding this book in your hands, you've already made a commitment to improving your store by improving yourself. And the good news about retailing is that there are plenty of other books out there to help you, in addition to this one. In fact, Mister Goodnews has a few suggestions in Appendix A.

Don't regard these weightier tomes as book report assignments you've got to read cover-to-cover. Keep them on your desk to flip through the next time you're on hold with tech support because the POS system is on the blink. Sometimes the most useful work is done during down time. And sometimes, as the owners of Flying Pig Children's Books found out, your best employees can come from the unlikeliest places.

> Prices aside, the main difference between one store and another is the people who work there.

Specialist Spotlight on

Flying Pig Children's Books

B abe, Olivia, Toot and Puddle, Pigling Bland, the entire cast of Swine Lake... and, of course, Charlotte. There's certainly no shortage of pig tales out there. And don't the owners of Flying Pig Children's Books in the hamlet of Charlotte, Vermont, know it!

For independent booksellers Elizabeth Bluemle and Josie Leavitt, there's nothing like seeing a child's face light up after she discovers the magic of a good story. "I cherish the sight of a child hugging a book as they exclaim, 'I love this!,'" says Elizabeth, who worked as a private school librarian in New York City before deciding with Josie, an English teacher herself (and award-winning stand-up comic), to escape the madness of Manhattan for the peace of Vermont.

After settling in and getting to know a few of their 3,000 or so fellow Charlotte residents, Elizabeth and Josie noticed a charming building for lease standing all by itself on the road that leads to the ferry back to Essex, New York. The building was so unique, they wanted to "save it from falling into the wrong hands," recalls Elizabeth.

The ladies first thought of opening a community center in the space, but then realized that, despite the ubiquitous Barnes & Noble and Borders in the area, not an independent bookstore could be found in their little town. A shop specializing in children's books it would be. With the famous Vermont Teddy Bear Company nearby and popular family bike routes in the area, they figured they'd have plenty of potential young customers.

What would *you* name a kids bookstore in a place called Charlotte? Charlotte's Web, of course. Unfortunately, locals pronounce it *Shar-LOT*. The partners just couldn't let go of the pig motif, though, and finally came up with one that flies, rather than just talks to spiders. Elizabeth says of Hamlet Phineas Philo, their perky porker mascot, "as long as the pig's flying, we're still here." Flying Pig Children's Books opened in late 1996.

With 33,000 items in about 850 square feet of actual selling space (and a roomy 150 square feet in back), you'd think pigs wouldn't be the only things flying around the little store. "Actually, it really has an airy feel to it," says Elizabeth, turning to a customer and asking, "Does it feel cramped in here?" The customer replies, "No. It's the *perfect* bookstore."

So perfect, it seems, that customers actually approach Elizabeth and Josie asking to work there.

At the start of their summer vacation in 2002, 13-year-old Nora and her 12-year-old sister Rose asked the Flying Pig's owners if they could "work" in the store. "They're such nice kids, we wanted to work out something," says Josie.

At first, she and Elizabeth weren't quite sure what to do with their eager "employees." They assigned them to shelve books. Though an important task, the girls quickly tired of the unglamorous side of bookselling. Enter the owners' clever plan to let Nora and Rose put their love of reading to work for the Flying Pig.

Nora and Rose would take a stack of five or six books at a time, read them cover to cover, and write reviews of each that were brief enough to fit on three-by-five index cards. Now, when a parent asks skeptically, "Just what is this book *The Sisterhood of the Traveling Pants* all about?" Elizabeth and Josie no longer have to summarize such oddly titled, popular teen novels in their own words. Handing the customer one of the girls' reviews, they can show mom or dad exactly what another young reader thought of the book.

> Handing the customer one of the girls' reviews, they can show mom or dad exactly what another young reader thought of the book.

Having a teacher assign *Treasure Island* or *Northanger Abbey* for class may elicit groans, but apparently teens will eagerly pick up the same books at a store — *if* recommended by one of their peers.

Elizabeth and Josie kept track of the girls' hours and paid them in books. They were so pleased with the results that they "hired" the sisters back this past summer. Although Josie notes that the idea of using young customers to create "shelf talkers" (the index cards used for the reviews) isn't unique to their store, the practice certainly seems unique to the industry. Bringing in your most devoted fans — your long-time customers — is "absolutely a plus," Josie says. And it's just the kind of sales strategy that independent specialists of all kinds could use.

Nora and Rose aren't the only long-time shoppers to come on board the Flying Pig staff. Elizabeth and Josie recently hired Jared, an avid and eclectic reader who'll work in the store part-time his senior year of high school. He's their first "after-school kid," Josie says. "He wrote an amazing cover letter."

Their first few years in business, Elizabeth and Josie struggled along as their only employees. By 2000, they had tired of working six days a week and had finally created two staff positions. When asked if she'd do anything differently were they starting over, Josie says without hesitation, "Hire a staff from the start." With Nora and Rose just starting high school, it looks like the Flying Pig has its summer team all set for the next few years, at least.

Y ou've assembled the best retail team this side of Abercrombie & Fitch. Now you're ready to go out and beat those superstores at their own game. Right? Wrong! Here's where most retail managers make their fatal mistake: assuming people can read their minds. How does little Johnny learn in the first grade not to pick his nose? Because someone has explained to him "we don't do that." Why did Susie stop eating paste? Because she was told not to… once, twice, maybe a hundred times. We don't expect our own flesh and blood to read our minds. Why do we think complete strangers off the street possess these magical powers?

Without any kind of training program in place, your "great new employees" will be no better than the ones you couldn't wait to get rid of. And I'm not just talking about refolding T-shirts into perfect rectangles, shelving books in subject order, or cleaning the customer bathroom the way mom would. I'm talking about basic manners. Things like smiling — genuinely — and nodding in acknowledgement when a new customer walks in, even if you're speaking with someone else. Making eye contact when you're talking to someone. Cutting inter-employee chitchat when ringing up a sale.

Jeez, that alone should set your store apart from the maddening crowd. How often do you deal with cashiers who spend the entire time ringing your order yackin' away with a co-worker? Does anyone actually think such behavior is polite? Of course not. But the "nobody told me I couldn't do that" defense lets these folks get away with it.

Look at your employees as blank computers that need the software for your personal "retail application" installed. I don't care where these folks worked before. Things are different here. There's one way to do things at your store — *your* way. As my friend Harry Friedman often

Chapter 5

The World According to You

says, "If your standards are negotiable, they're not standards." Yet most companies adhere to the Groucho axiom: "These are my standards. If you don't like them, I have others." And then those managers complain how difficult it is to get "good help."

Before you can actually train your people, however, you must know what you want them to do. Dust off that copy of *The World According to You* sitting somewhere in your desk — you know, those stapled-together pages otherwise known as a policy and procedure manual or an employee handbook.

Don't have one? That's even better news. As my dear editor tells me, sometimes it's just easier to start from scratch. This list of policy things now in your hands (or in your head) will tell every single person who comes to work for you exactly what you expect and how you expect it to be done. Let's start organizing them on paper:

STEP #1. The basics. Employee benefits and pay structure. Policies and guidelines on attendance, sexual harassment, and drug and alcohol use. Rules regarding employee safety. Any useful employee handbook will contain sections on such basics. Numerous articles and guides are available to help the small-business manager put together these relatively generic sections of your handbook. One of my favorite sources for legal assistance — much of it free — is the website www.nolo.com.

Employee handbooks should never imply a contract. So, before you forget, include a disclaimer on the first page stating that nothing in the handbook creates or implies an employment contract.

STEP #2. Industry-specific tasks. A cycling shop requires specific rules for demonstrating bikes. Say your state has a helmet law and you allow employees to help kids try out bikes in your back parking area. You'd better be darn sure you put in writing that all children trying out bikes on company premises must wear properly fitting helmets. If you manage a bookstore, you probably want your employees to unpack books a certain way — without stabbing a box cutter into their covers or opening a vein, for instance. Hearing the responsible employee say "Nobody told me..." isn't going to help when you're facing a lawsuit after a helmetless five-year-old goes noggin-over-kiester into your dumpster. Nor will muttered apologies bring much comfort to a line of 10-year-olds eyeing shredded copies of the latest Harry Potter tome.

STEP #3. Job-specific tasks. Your sales team must know not only how to ring up sales, check prices, and place special orders, but little tasks like changing the paper in the register. Your back office folks need to know how to match invoices to packing slips or purchase orders, your coding system, and how to determine which invoices get paid first to take advantage of early-pay discounts. If your employees find themselves on the other end of the phone with a customer, do they know what to say, or do they just hit the "hold" button?

The good news is that Step #3 is easier in a sense than Step #2 (at least as far as the main staff goes) because you can delegate some of the writing to top team members who actually know how to do these things. Some specialist retailers I know even let their employees write each other's job descriptions. That's a good exercise in teamwork — and a *great* way to find out why certain things might not be getting done around your place.

STEP #4. General maintenance tasks. Picking up cigarette butts in the parking lot. Cleaning the restroom. Removing finger goo from the displays. Ugh! All the stuff we star salespeople think we're above doing.

> Some specialist retailers I know even let their employees write each other's job descriptions.

The superstores can afford nightly cleaning crews to handle such chores. Independent specialists usually can't. The contract for a cleaning crew can run you thousands a month — money much better spent on advertising, general maintenance, or just added to the bottom line. Unless you've got a place the size of a Wal-Mart, your team should be able to keep your store presentable in the downtime between the throngs of customers. (And if you're never without throngs of customers, you can probably afford that nightly cleaning crew.)

STEP #5. Your personal retail gripes. This is the fun one! Make mental notes for a month about each poor customer service experience you have at another retail location — specialists and superstores alike.

Wandering around a home improvement store for hours in search of some form of life... standing half-clothed in a dressing room waiting desperately for a salesperson to come fetch you a different size... finding the supersized detergent box was packed on top of your eggs and strawberries.... We've all experienced these shopping frustrations.

Then get your people involved. Order in from a favorite delivery place, take 'em to lunch, whatever.... Just get your team relaxed and feeling appreciated and start asking about their own worst retail experiences — as *customers*, not as retail employees. This is not the time to level criticism about anything going on in your own store or anywhere else they may have worked. This is the time to complain about everyone else!

At the end of this gripe session, you should have a list of Things Customers Hate. Then ask for suggestions about how to ensure that none of your store's customers suffers similar treatment. The rules you end up putting in writing will probably be pretty simple, since in most cases we're talking about common courtesy.

But the key here is that you've had your people come up with the rules themselves, based on their own experiences being ignored, insulted, isolated, infuriated, invalidated, and generally trodden under the feet of retailers who completely take them and their money for granted.

STEP #6. Take a deep breath. Seriously. I'm not expecting you to get all this done in a single afternoon, or a single month. The complete process of putting everything in writing could take upwards of a year — but next year will be here as quickly as the last one left. Start with the basics and keep adding on.

STEP #7. Have employees read your handbook and acknowledge that they understand it. As you complete each section or new draft of your employee handbook, distribute copies to your team. Give them time to read it and ask questions. Then have them sign statements that they understand its contents. Put those statements in each of their files.

Good job so far. But just because you've got your policies and expectations in writing doesn't mean you've taken charge of your store. An employee who signs a statement that he understands the rules is not the same as an employee who has been trained to follow them.

I remember the day, years ago, that my eight-year-old son taught me this lesson. I'd asked him to clean up his room. He scowled and stomped off. Ten minutes later he was back in front of the television. "I thought I told you to clean up your room," I said, calculating that it would have taken me the better part of an hour to do the job. "I did," he replied. "Let's go see," says me.

The room still looked like the aftermath of a rock concert at the Coliseum. "This isn't clean!" I bellowed. "Yes it is," the little guy

> Just because you've got your policies and expectations in writing doesn't mean you've taken charge of your store.

protested. "So what did you *do?*" I demanded. "I picked up all the trash and put it in the can," he said.

Epiphany! I never told the child what I consider "clean." My definition includes tasks like returning the entire wardrobe from the floor to the closet and so forth. But an eight-year-old boy's? Throwing away last week's uneaten grilled cheese sandwich, apparently. It seems I was not a very good leader when it came to managing my boy. I assumed he was as good a mind reader as the rest of my employees.

That was the day I realized the importance of the Show Me Game. It's a simple game, with few rules. It works just as well with new employees as with current team members (in your store *or* your family) who need a little refresher course in how things are done *your* way. Let's start by playing Show Me with some of your current team players.

Alex keeps ringing up cash sales as "create invoice," a command that tells your computer software program to bill the customer. At the end of the day, Alex's cash drawer always has too much unidentified money in it. The accounting department goes bonkers when they start reconciliations. You've determined that he's failing to operate the system correctly because he must have forgotten how — *not* because he's unwilling.

This is no time for a reprimand. It's time for the Show Me Game. Pull him aside and walk through the process of ringing up a regular sale. Explain the importance to the store's overall operation of doing the task this way. Alex needs to know which cog in your little retail wheel he represents. When you're finished, ask: "Do you understand?"

The answer will always be "yes." You can usually hear the B.B.s rolling around inside your employees' heads as they nod. Why do people refuse to admit they're confused? It must have something to do with men not wanting to ask directions. It's up to you to find out whether Alex is agreeing out of convenience, or because he truly understands what you just told him.

How do you do this? Just say: "Terrific! Show me!" If Alex can repeat the instructions, you know he can execute them. The next time he rings up a sale incorrectly, you may consider it an infraction, because *you* know that *he* knows the "hows" and "whys" of the process.

If he repeats the directions incorrectly, however, you have the opportunity to correct his behavior on the spot. Just tell him he's close and walk through the process once more. "Now do you understand?" "Yes." "Great! Show me." Repeat the process until he's got it.

You've just removed the roadblock. Alex now knows what you expect and how to make you happy. Yet as simple as this game sounds, how many managers out there actually handle problem employees like this?

Try an example from the salesfloor. (Remember, sales are the easiest things to manage because the numbers — the data *things* — always tell the story.) You've got the top specialist camera store in town and, in terms of pure numbers, Francis is one of your top salespeople. But your sales records from the last few months indicate that he has sold almost no accessories. You realize the guy is failing in this regard because he doesn't seem to remember how to do add-ons effectively — not because he's unwilling to make more money both for himself and for the store.

So (in private) tell him: "Francis, this report shows you're missing a terrific opportunity with camera bag accessories."

> You have the opportunity to correct his behavior on the spot.

This alerts him to the good news that there's more money to be made. With the right tone and a non-confrontational manner, you needn't provide the translation: "Francis, you're not pulling your weight in this particular category."

Just telling him he's short of the mark is not going to make him a better salesperson, however. He's not selling accessories because something is wrong: Either he doesn't know how to do effective add-ons, or he doesn't want to. If he doesn't know how, the Show Me Game will teach him. If he doesn't want to — perhaps he feels it makes him a "pushy salesman" — you can deal with that, too.

Picture me, the new regional sales director for a major electronics firm. The company president handed me a list of my job responsibilities. Imagine my horror at realizing that I, the master salesman, only knew how to do about half of the items on the list. I didn't even know what the others meant!

But I never said a word. I didn't want the president to think he hired the wrong guy. I suffered through a year of figuring out (on my own) how to do the other half of the list. I could have been at full speed from day one had my boss taken the time to play a few rounds of the Show Me Game.

A new employee needs to feel productive the first day. So, to make the Show Me Game easier, cut and paste the store-specific tasks from your employee handbook into a document I like to call the "New Employee's Survival Guide." To the right of each task, put a place to check off and initial that the employee has been trained in and learned that task.

At the end of the list, leave a signature and date line so that each new employee can put in writing that he has mastered the above tasks of specialist retailing *your* way. When the list has been completely checked off and the document signed, you have the right to expect results from that new team member.

As time-consuming as writing handbooks and drafting training lists are, this is the easy part. The hard part is *your commitment to do the training*. You'll have to sit with each new employee from now on and train him, line by line, playing Show Me all the way to the end. This is the best way to get your people up to speed. But I guarantee you, that new employee will be delighted someone is taking the time to help him succeed.

One tip: Don't try to cram too much into someone's head at one time. You want these folks to feel good about the fact that they made the move to your store, not overwhelmed. Depending on your specific market category and the size of your staff, the training process can take as little as a week or as long as several months. Simplify things by making the training subjects relevant to each other: all the counter stuff, all the stock room stuff, all the HR policies, all the opening and closing chores, et cetera.

Now, I bet you'll have such good results with your new employees that you'll wish you could retrain all your current staff members. Well, go ahead! At least a few of your team players will breathe a sigh of relief: "Thank goodness someone is finally defining my job."

Others will resist. They've been doing things their way for years. Why should they play this silly game of Show Me? But if your veteran team members won't do things the way you want them to, the new guys have no reason to either. If — after including your employees' input *à la* Step #5 above and walking everyone through the "whys" as well as the "hows" — you've got some old-timers who just won't

> I guarantee you, that new employee will be delighted someone is taking the time to help him succeed.

change, I think you know what needs to be done. Either you're in charge, or they are.

Okay, okay, I know... This all sounds great on paper. But we live in the real world, Pollyanna! We busy managers don't have time for all this training. We're too busy staying one step ahead of the big-box retailers. What can I say? That's the trick: *You, the manager, just have to manage it.*

If yours is a small establishment and you're the only one who can do the training, so be it. Just do a little every day, or every week. Don't try to accomplish this all at once. You'll stress yourself out and quit the project, if not specialist retailing altogether. (And we hapless customers, tired of the superstore short shrift, definitely don't want that.) If you have managers under you, play the training and Show Me Game with them... and then send them off to do the same with the rest of the team.

Plenty of business books out there will promise you great results overnight. The GOOD NEWS ABOUT RETAILING books are not among them. What I can promise you is: *This process of training your people is not easy.* What's easy is to do what you've been doing for years. But if that worked, you wouldn't need to change — and you wouldn't have committed to taking charge of your store's future by buying this book.

It's time for a little congratulations... for you, and for your team. You've made a commitment to change, and your employees have — at the very least — made a commitment to join the team of an independent specialist at a time when many consider independent specialists an endangered species. Thank them!

We all know that praise is fun to give and fun to receive. In fact, in many cases it's better than money. That award for employee of the week, month, or year can go further than a little bonus cash. Not a lot further, but some.

And praise is especially effective when earned as the result of a teaching session. You trained Alex to do what·you wanted, he did it correctly, you praised him, and now he's jazzed about his job.

Just keep in mind that you should never tell someone he did a good job without giving the details: "Alex, I'd like to compliment you on your new computer skills. I haven't heard your name spoken in anger by the accounting department all week. Your cash drawer reconciles, and the books come out clean every night. Way to go. Thanks." Acknowledging the details makes it clear you're paying attention.

So… great job! You've made it through my lectures on managing people by managing data, incentive-based pay programs, and hands-on training techniques like the Show Me Game — and now you're starting to take charge of your store.

Acknowledging
the details
makes it clear
you're paying
attention.

Specialist Spotlight on

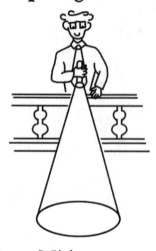

Midwest Mountaineering

If Indiana Jones ever opened a retail store for the outdoorsman, I'm sure it would look just like Midwest Mountaineering. His name would be different, of course…. Perhaps Minneapolis Jones, after the specialist retailer's location. But more likely it would be Rod Johnson.

Like Indy, Rod is an adventurous man who lives to explore exotic and out-of-the-way places. Immediately after earning an undergraduate degree in chemistry in 1969, he decided to see if he could travel around the world on a dollar a day. (In those days, a dollar really *was* a dollar. A gallon of gas was 22 cents.) Over the years, he's toured the Amazon in the jungles of Peru, floated up the fabled Nile, and climbed Mt. Kilimanjaro in the heart of Africa.

His passion for the adventurous life stemmed from childhood. Rod's parents took him and two younger siblings camping twice a month while he was growing up. In the Boy Scouts, he worked his way up to Eagle status. The great outdoors was not his only interest, though. Young Minneapolis Jones had a serious business streak, too. He collected and traded coins, buying them from friends and selling them at a profit. He won a tape recorder (big doings by the standards of the day) for selling the most subscriptions as a paperboy. And he did particularly well selling fire extinguishers.

"I'd start a small fire on their front porch and then ring the doorbell," says Rod, who carried a baking pan and gasoline as his sales props. "When they answered the door, I asked them if they were protected against fires." Perhaps — but who would protect them against Rod?!

After the first installment of Rod's around-the-world venture, he tried his hand at several jobs, including an attempt to clean up as a vacuum cleaner salesman. That wasn't quite the sweep he thought it would be, and, since there was no chemistry between him and his chosen topic of study at school, he decided to merge his business instincts with his love of the outdoor life. In 1970, Midwest Mountaineering was born.

Now there was no actual outdoor retail industry in those days. Manufacturers were happy to sell to anyone who would give them an order. So, in true entrepreneurial fashion, Rod launched his outfitting company at the kitchen table. In six months, he needed a storefront. Unfortunately, things weren't much easier with a retail roof over his head. If Rod had to go to lunch, use the john, or run some errands, he put a "closed" sign in the window. The few retail customers he *did* have weren't too happy. Rod needed an employee.

That was 33 years ago. His first month in business, Rod grossed $50 with no employees. Last December, he grossed $500,000 with 120 (70 regular and 50 seasonal workers). Way to go, Rod!

Rod's sense of adventure has encouraged him to do many outstanding things over the years that have contributed to his success. For one, he can count on his profit margins. He refuses to match a price from REI, which has two stores nearby, or Galyans, a big-box retailer with three locations in his area (80,000 square feet or more each). The team at Midwest Mountaineering offers service and serious advice. Rod thinks that's worth something, and obviously his customers agree. The store also carries high-end products the superstores simply cannot sell. When you're getting $400 for just the shell of a hiking jacket, you need a specialist to explain its value.

Rod's employees are passionate outdoorsy types, so he has little trouble with turnover. In fact, many of his part-time employees have full-time jobs elsewhere. They work for Midwest because they love outdoor

> When you're getting $400 for just the shell of a hiking jacket, you need a specialist to explain its value.

sports, and the products that help people enjoy them. Rod has more than a dozen employees who've worked for him for more than a dozen years each. That says a lot. I've always said you can tell the quality of management by the seniority of the staff. Apparently, Midwest Mountaineering is a really nice place to work.

The store does have some theft, but not as much as other specialist retailers. There's not really a resale market for outdoor gear, so anything that's stolen is for the employee's personal use. After much deliberation, Rod did keep up with the times by installing security cameras starting in 1999, first in the front and then in the backroom areas.

Another of his adventurous policies is his compensation program. Rod's salespeople receive an hourly wage plus spiffs, the office folks are on salary, and *everyone* participates in Midwest Mountaineering's profit-sharing program in the years there are profits to be shared. A third of the profits go back into the company, a third go to Rod, and a third go to his team of dedicated employees. He notes that there have been some years when his people have gotten some "very nice bonuses."

But the most adventurous move Rod has made has to do with his employee handbook — or handbooks, to be more accurate. Like all retailers, Rod realized after a few years in business that he should have his store policies and procedures in writing.

"If people aren't sure what you want them to do," he says, "they can push the boundaries a little too much." So he and his managers used a standard HR guidelines book to create their first employee manual. Then, about 10 years ago, he split the handbook's contents into three separate guides: a "Store Procedures Manual," a "Cashier Manual," and an "Employee Handbook."

The first includes sections on "The Basics" (how to greet customers; how to suggest additional merchandise) and "Policies and Procedures" (how to take down written telephone messages; the importance of a quiet cash register area; policies for selling knives, dealing with unsupervised children, and handling in-store photo shoots). Separate sections cover internal security (rules intended to prevent employee theft), store security (handling shoplifters), and an entire easy-to-read section on filling out the various Midwest Mountaineering forms.

The "Cashier Manual" addresses those tasks specific to the job category, from layaways and rentals to phone orders and mistendering. Polite dealings with customers should never take back seat to policy and procedure, Rod is careful to note. The manual begins: "[This] is the basic written 'how-to' for cashiers, but it is by no means exhaustive. If you have any further questions, please ask the Head Cashier or Bookkeepers. Most importantly, be friendly. Cashiers are the first and last employees the customers see in the store."

The "Employee Handbook" is the most general of the three manuals and contains all of the legally required "small print" about sexual harassment in the workplace, the company's no-drug-use policy, et cetera. Many employee handbooks kick off with all the things you are *not allowed to do* once you join the company. Rod arranged his handbook with all the benefits of working at his store right up front: wages (including advances), retirement and savings programs, medical coverage, sponsored store trips and free demo gear (in a section called "Continuing Education"), and "The Extras" (subsidized parking, bike storage, employee holds and layaways). What a positive approach!

Dividing all this material into separate manuals "seemed like an easy distinction to make," says Rod. Unfortunately, the more successful

> Rod arranged his employee handbook with all the benefits of working at his store right up front.

Midwest Mountaineering became, the more rules he needed. The size of the manuals was no longer the main issue — it was their timeliness. They were always out of date, and it was costing a fortune to keep reprinting them. So Rod joined the 21st century and put his employee manuals online.

When a new employee joins Rod's team, she receives an e-mail with a link to the intranet site where Midwest Mountaineering's three manuals are posted (to see the employee homepage and the table of contents for all the three handbooks, visit http://mail.midwestmtn.com/employee/intranet/).

Accessing the intranet site triggers a notification to the human resources manager, who then brings an acknowledgment form over for the new employee to sign. That form is placed into the employee's permanent file. To encourage new staff members to access the rules and regulations site quickly, Rod has made activation of a new employee's staff discount contingent upon reading and acknowledging the pertinent intranet pages.

So, what's next for Minneapolis Jones? Rod is an inventor. He just applied for patents on a survival vest and a — guess what?! — tankless toilet. With the tankless toilet, consumers will never again have to run upstairs and jiggle the handle to keep it from running continually. The survival vest? Well, put it on and go a' hiking. It contains everything from a tent to a GPS locater in a lightweight piece of clothing. It would have been the perfect item for Indiana Jones.

And the best part? Indy would have paid retail.

Chapter 6
Crime and Punishment

Okay, you've done everything right. You've written a handbook and played Show Me with your employees at every turn. You've coached them until you're all comatose. And still, one person is not responding. It happens. He either still doesn't know how to do the task or just doesn't want to. You want him to succeed, but you can't be expected to single him out as a career project. It's time for another powerful motivation technique: write him up!

"Are you telling me that writing people up will motivate them to become what I need?" I sure am. Subordinates, like all children, need to know where the lines are drawn. Yet who among us has not desperately looked around for something "more important" to do in the hopes that the problem will correct itself? It never does — it always gets worse.

The prospect of confronting an employee is not a happy one. We fear anger, lies, self-defense moves on both sides, and, inevitably, hard feelings. It's okay to be uncomfortable. But uncomfortable does not mean "bail out." It means "be careful." And being careful as a manager means understanding the concept of progressive discipline.

Progressive discipline typically goes like this: one verbal warning, followed by two written warnings, and then, when all else fails, termination.[2] This process gets your message through your employee's thick noggin and guarantees you that the problem child can never say, "Nobody ever told me." Take note that verbal warnings should be spelled out in writing immediately and included in the employee's permanent file. The good news is that for most people, a verbal warning is all they'll ever need.

---

[2] Serious infractions such as violent behavior or theft are obviously cause for immediate dismissal. If you simply issue a warning to someone who behaves violently, you're setting yourself up for a lawsuit if there is a second incident in which the employee harms another worker or a customer.

Once you're ready to talk with your employee, this is what you do:

STEP #1. Get your facts in order. Pull copies of any previous reprimands from the employee's file and assemble any documentation related to the current infraction.

You gave Anita a verbal warning three months ago and a written warning a month later that she was violating store policy by not checking the identification of credit card customers. Now you find out that she accepted a card for a $15 sale, the card turned out to be stolen, and your merchant services company is refusing to pay because she didn't check ID. Gather the previous warnings, the receipt from the bad sale, and correspondence from your financial institution.

STEP #2. Call the employee into your office. Never, ever reprimand an employee in front of co-workers. It's humiliating for her and makes you look like a jerk.

STEP #3. State the problem.

"Anita, I've reminded you twice in the past that store policy requires an identification check for all credit card purchases. Last week you accepted what turned out to be a stolen credit card without asking for ID. The store is now out $15 plus the cost of the merchandise."

STEP #4. Review the reasons for the rule. Show the advantage of following the rules and/or the hardship caused when the rules are broken.

"We can prevent stolen card sales by properly checking ID. This saves us money. It also gives our regular customers additional confidence in us as a business. We are demonstrating with each purchase that we care about their financial protection, as well as our own."

STEP #5. Write the infraction on your "Employee Interview Form" (see Appendix B) **and the reason the infraction is a hardship.**

"Anita rang up a $15 credit card sale without checking for customer identification. The card was stolen, and the bank is contesting payment."

STEP #6. Write down the course of action needed to correct the situation. You're giving the employee a second, or third, chance. It's also a good idea to ask the employee if there is any additional support or training she feels she could use.

"Anita will review the store's sales-register process with the assistant manager immediately. They will both sign the training form that the review has been done and that the steps involved were understood."

STEP #7. Write down what will happen if the infraction is repeated. It is essential that you document such a warning in writing.

"A repetition of the infraction will be cause for immediate dismissal — regardless of whether the credit card used in the transaction is stolen or legitimate."

STEP #8. Neither whining nor tears nor clever excuses should sway you from your position. Although it's smart to let the employee tell her side of the story at some point during this process, do not let emotional pleas or feeble excuses change your mind. This is the hardest part, I know. But, unless Anita is dumber than the proverbial doorknob, she knows she's screwing up, she knows she's costing the store money and she knows she deserves to lose her job if she does it again. Picture your good employees standing next to Anita as she snivels, their faces crestfallen as you tell them you can't afford raises because you can barely afford to keep the lights on. Then say calmly:

Neither whining nor tears nor clever excuses should sway you from your position.

"Anita, I've reminded you twice in the past that store policy requires an identification check for all credit card purchases. You have now cost the store $75 plus the cost of the merchandise. I hope you will take this third warning seriously. I cannot have one employee costing the company so much money."

STEP #9. Have the employee sign the form. That interview form is now very important data — data that will save you a ton of grief if you end up firing the employee and she takes you to court. Do note, however, that the employee is signing that she *understands* what the two of you have talked about, not that she necessarily *agrees* with it.

Now, you're an experienced manager. You can see that your counterpart in the above scenario would have to fire Anita eventually. So why wait until she screws up again, possibly costing the company many hundreds of dollars the next time? Because the process of progressive discipline is important for two reasons.

First, it protects you should the employee ever take you to court: You can document that you gave the employee multiple warnings that she was doing something wrong. Second, it gives that employee multiple chances to start doing things right. Everyone deserves a second chance, and sometimes a potentially excellent employee needs a third or fourth.

The key thing to remember is that you must maintain control of the situation when confronting rule infractions — regardless of whether the employee is clearly headed for termination, like Anita, or just needs a little reminder to stop testing the limits.

Let's consider one more quick example, more typical of the everyday kinds of problems managers face than the extreme of the credit card and IDs situation:

You: "Frank, you've been late three times this week: Monday, Tuesday, and today. [There's your data.] When you're late, your co-workers have to pick up the slack and still get their own work done. There's one less body to answer the phone and wait on customers. This costs the store a fortune. That's why you can't come in late."

Frank: "There was an accident the size of New Jersey on the freeway. You'll see it on the news tonight."

You: "I understand. You've been late three times this week: Monday, Tuesday, and today. When you're late, everyone else has to pick up your slack and still get their own work done. There's one less body to answer the phone and wait on customers. This costs the store a fortune. That's why you can't come in late."

Frank: "Yeah, I know. It's not my fault. I'm trying to get someone to fix the car now. I haven't been feeling well."

You: "I understand. You've been late three times this week. When you're late, everyone else has to pick up your slack and still get their own work done. There's one less body to answer the phone and wait on customers. This costs the store a fortune. That's why you can't come in late."

Frank: "It won't happen again."

You: "Thank you."

I'm *not* asking you to have no feelings. I'm asking you to control the meeting. Don't allow Frank to change the subject. You're calling him on his lateness because the problem is chronic — it happens over and over

> I'm *not* asking you to have no feelings. I'm asking you to control the meeting.

again. We all know the difference between chronic behavior and an ice storm that knocks down power lines and prevents half of your city from getting to work. If you let an employee off the hook for being life's victim, you're asking for more trouble. Waver from your position, and your effectiveness as a manager is over. Your employees will have taken charge of your store.

Before we turn to our SPECIALIST SPOTLIGHT on Blue Ridge Mountain Sports, I've got a few more tips to help you take charge — and keep charge — of employee behavior at your store:

Stay on topic. Don't soften a criticism by telling the person how good he is in other areas. "Frank, I'm surprised you continue to come in late, because you're a darn good salesperson once you get out on that floor." Say something like that and I guarantee you the only thing Frank leaves your office with is: "The boss thinks I'm a darn good salesperson."

Remind the employee that actions have consequences. For most managers, telling an employee that his actions will have consequences means you have to threaten to fire him. Nothing could be further from the truth. The most obvious consequence to him violating the rule again is another write-up. Then there are all those nasty chores around the place that need to be done, many of which are worse than being fired. How about a week's worth of parking lot or restroom duty? You've got all kinds of alternatives to termination. Be creative, but be fair. In most cases, you don't really want the employee to leave. You just want him to change his behavior. But remember...

Never offer a consequence you're not willing to follow through on. If you tell Anita she'll be fired for violating the ID policy one more time, you must fire her when it happens. If you tell Frank he'll get restroom-cleaning duty for a week the next time he's late, you must give it to him. You have no choice. If you don't follow through on your words, the rest of your people will never take you seriously again. You might as well retire now.

It's easy to let things slide. He's only 10 minutes late.... She didn't check ID but the credit card was legitimate.... Keeping the big picture in mind makes it easier to confront these little violations when they occur. *The World According to You* is not an arbitrary set of rules and expectations. It's your vision for running an independent retail store in a manner that will encourage customers to shop, buy, and develop a fierce loyalty to your place.

Unless they need hot dogs for a Brownie troop or toilet paper by the pallet, most customers do not shop simply on price. They want good value and plain, old-fashioned courtesy. Unlike the big-box retailers, an independent's more manageable size means you can see that such personal attention is exactly what your customers get.

The World According to You is not an arbitrary set of rules and expectations.

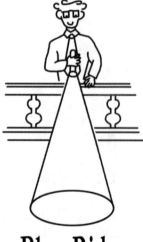

Specialist Spotlight on

Blue Ridge Mountain Sports

"Take a hike!" Those are words Stephen Nauss can be heard telling customers on a regular basis. "But before you take that hike," adds the owner of Blue Ridge Mountain Sports, "let me sell you all the things you're going to need on the way." Steve's 13-store specialty chain scattered across the Mid-Atlantic states is just the kind of outdoor sporting goods place Teddy Roosevelt would have gloried in before setting off on one of his wilderness adventures.

Just as Teddy's childhood, spent surrounded by nature, profoundly affected his adulthood interests, eight years at summer camp as a child instilled in Steve a deep love of nature and an appreciation for the health an outdoor lifestyle affords.

In fact, it was Steve's fascination with the natural process that probably sent him to college with an interest in studying pre-med. After earning his undergraduate degree in psychology at the University of Virginia in 1972, however, he decided to skip med school altogether. Heading to the woods near Hanover, New Hampshire, he spent the next several months camping while hoping a vision of his future would reveal itself.

Returning to civilization, Steve joined a friend who was managing an outdoor equipment shop in Westchester County, outside New York City. Fresh from his recent union with nature, Steve thought a job selling backpacks and hiking gear would be fun while he considered grad school. Like many who wander into retailing, he thought he was just passing through.

Soon after, a college friend invited him to join his two-store operation back in Charlottesville, Virginia. Blue Ridge Mountain Sports, open just about a year, wasn't doing too well. Like many start-ups, the business was undercapitalized. In no time, Steve was managing one of the two stores and acting as buyer for both. "I enjoy running the numbers," he soon discovered. So Steve decided in 1973 to buy into the company, rounded up six investors and slowly turned Blue Ridge into a successful retail chain. Partners came and went as the years passed until, by 1996, Steve was sole owner.

After more than two decades in retail, Steve wanted a rest. Besides, "my wife said I wasn't smiling enough anymore," he recalls. So he sold Blue Ridge and spent the next two years with his wife, three kids, and the golf course. "But how much golf can you play?" he asks. "I got bored."

Funny how things work out: Just about the time Steve was finding retirement a little dull, the new owner of Blue Ridge was having trouble making ends meet. So in 1998, Steve bought back his old business.

Under his expert direction, the specialist chain prospered once again. Blue Ridge now has more products, more visibility, and more employees than ever before. During the holidays and for special events, Steve's staff reaches 400 or more; his core team is about 120 part- and full-time workers.

Keeping all of those people toeing the company line starts with plenty of training — both in-house and with outside consultants — and with the Blue Ridge policy manual. Once new employees sign the manual acceptance form, Steve considers them responsible for the manual's contents.

Distributing the details of the "hows" and "whys" of running things at Blue Ridge *his* way is not the difficult part for Steve. The challenge is disciplining employees who run afoul of the rules, when yours is no longer a two-store enterprise.

> The challenge is disciplining employees who run afoul of the rules, when yours is no longer a two-store enterprise.

Fortunately, Steve has grown philosophical as his company has grown in size: There are the rules of management... and then there's real life. And in real life, it's difficult to get boardroom policy down to the sales-floor. "But if you're confident you are doing the best you can, and you don't let up, you'll do just fine," he says.

With 13 stores, getting a dozen or so managers to follow his lead in doling out employee discipline can be a real challenge. Doing the best *he* can means that Steve has established an impressive training program for his management staff.

All new managers head first to the company headquarters in Charlottesville, just up the way from the chain's flagship store, for three to four days of training. If the new manager requires more experience or tutelage in a specific area, he is then sent to the store in the chain where they do that specific thing best.

"We do not have cookie-cutter stores," Steve says. "They range in size from 2,000 to 8,000 square feet, and because of that, each store's merchandising and management challenges are very different."

To keep his managers in top form, Steve holds an annual retreat, renting several beach houses in Corolla, North Carolina, for three or four days. Mornings are dedicated to serious work: At a recent retreat, Steve hired an HR attorney to teach his managers about the latest employee hiring, performance review, and disciplinary requirements. Afternoons are unstructured, with activities on the agenda like trying out new kayaks and other equipment.

In addition to his extensive and ongoing training program, Steve employs an operations manager to act as a physical liaison between himself and his numerous managers. Not that Steve has an aversion to face-to-face meetings with his people — in fact, he encourages managers to walk in or phone as often as they wish with requests for advice or assistance... and they do. It's just that it's a little difficult for Steve to be at all 13 of his stores at once.

The operations manager, who conducts all manager reviews and follows up with the store managers on issues of policy and procedure, visits each store on a rotating basis. Any store manager who could use the advice or assistance of Blue Ridge's top brass — but doesn't want to discuss things on the phone or via e-mail — knows that Steve's right-hand representative is probably already on his way.

One store in particular is a little out of the way for Steve to visit often. The Blue Ridge location in the winter resort area of Wintergreen, Virginia, is swamped with customers during the cold weather months. Come summer, though, and the employees there couldn't be more bored. Now, bored employees are not good news. "As they say, idle hands are the devil's workshop," notes Steve.

So he and his management team devised a creative solution. Camp Jeep, a four-day event sponsored by DaimlerChrysler near Wintergreen every summer, draws 8,000 people and 3,000 Jeeps. And it turns out that folks who like Jeeps like all kinds of outdoor sporting activities. The Blue Ridge staff set up a retail store on the event premises and made a killing.

The scale of the problem may be greater, but the basics of smart management are the same as when Steve was just starting out. And sticking with what works is the same tactic Steve adopts when confronted with big-box dealers coming onto his home turf.

Sticking with what works is the same tactic Steve adopts when confronted with big-box dealers.

"Keep playing the game the way you've always played it," he says. "If you try to play the game the way they play it, you'll get killed. True, you'll lose some business at first when they move in. But after a year or so, you'll have all your old customers back."

And it's a funny thing.... His customers keep coming back, and Steve keeps telling them to take a hike. Go figure!

H ey, boss! How am I doing?" Even if you've never had an employee say this to you, I promise you they're *all* thinking it. Everyone wants to know if they're on track, if the boss likes them, if they have a future with the company…. And the funny thing is that, while your employees are worrying about their own futures, you're probably concerned about the same thing: How will my team succeed — or fail — next week, next quarter, next year…? Regularly scheduled employee performance reviews provide both sides the opportunity for just such a discussion. In fact, the give-and-take of such meetings is so essential that I prefer to call them performance *interviews*.

An interview allows both parties to express themselves. Your team members need to know how they're doing, what you expect from them, and what they'll get if they continue to perform as they have been. Coaches don't send athletes into a game without feedback and a pep talk, do they?

We all know that the very phrase "employee review" fills most people with angst. But have you ever thought about just why this is? The reason is that, at most workplaces, the review (capital "R") is the one time every year that the employee sits down with his boss and finds out how he's been screwing up. Sometimes, the employee is pretty sure what the boss thinks he's been doing wrong for the last 12 months (even if he doesn't agree with it). And sometimes, any criticism of the employee comes to him as a complete surprise. In either case, this is just wrong, wrong, *wrong!*

Did I mention this is wrong?

You can lose a lot of business — *and* cause a lot of unnecessary stress and unhappiness in both your own life and your employee's — if you

Chapter 7
The Dreaded Employee Review

wait six or 12 months before addressing a problem. It's human nature to put off unpleasant situations. But we learned earlier why *managers absolutely must face problems head on*. You cannot fume silently every time Anita processes a credit card without ID or Frank saunters in late... and then blow up and fire them for violating store policy without warning.

First of all, it's unhealthy. You don't need another ulcer. Second, it could land you in legal hot water. Do you think the progressive discipline process was invented by a manager with too much time on his hands? Progressive discipline — one verbal warning, two written warnings, then the oh-so-satisfactory sacking — is the result of years of clever thinking by employers trying to deal with the legal ramifications of (largely successful) lawsuits by disgruntled employees. The good news is that, *if* you're now following my advice about employee discipline from Chapter Six, your regular employee reviews really won't be the awful encounters you imagine them to be.

That said, I'd like to go over a few points about what makes an effective Employee Performance Interview:

TIP #1. Focus on the data, not the person.

To be both effective and legal, a review must focus on data, not opinions. When reviewing a salesperson, talk about the numbers. When reviewing a bookkeeper, talk about the state of payables versus receivables. Deliver your comments matter-of-factly, and bring any supporting documentation with you — sales reports, timesheets, P&Ls, whatever.

When offering praise, give examples; otherwise, it's just an empty stroke: "Sally, you're doing a great job this quarter. Your overall sales are up 27%. Most of that has come from your add-ons. You haven't been late for work either, and that takes a lot of the stress off the rest of the staff. I like that. Thanks." Sally has no doubt you know what you're talking about and that you're not just giving false praise. This is not just your opinion. Sally *is* doing well.

The same holds true when you deliver a negative report: "George, you're selling 21% fewer accessories this quarter than last. That's not the direction we want to see for you. Let's figure out how we can help you get back on track." Don't ask George what he is going to do about it. If he knew what to do, wouldn't he already be doing it? The question itself makes things awkward.

If you state the facts, and *only* the facts, your employees will never have a valid reason to resent you. You are simply reading back their performance data. You didn't make this stuff up.

TIP #2. Prepare standard evaluation forms — and use them.

Appendix B includes a basic Employee Interview Form, which can be tailored to each department and/or job position at your company. Sections II and III on this sample form apply to all employees. You must tailor the evaluation points in Section I, however, to fit each job category on your staff list. The criteria by which you judge an assistant sales manager's performance will differ from the criteria for an administrative job, for example. The list of criteria for each job should match the job description for that position.

TIP #3. Tell your employees what YOU want from them.

Again, not only is this smart management, in many cases it is legally advisable. If you never tell an employee what you expect of him, you

> If you state the facts, and *only* the facts, your employees will never have a valid reason to resent you.

cannot be disappointed when he doesn't live up to your expectations. Remember the story about my son's definition of a "clean room"? Employees can't read your mind any better than kids can.

The performance interview should cover not only what you want from the employee now — in other words, what his current job duties are and how he is fulfilling them — but what you are looking for in the future. What sales goals should the employee aim for in the next six months? What new accounting processes do you want implemented by the end of the next quarter?

Help your people succeed by giving them concrete goals.

Tip #4. Ask your employees what THEY want from you.

Encourage them to ask what they expect from your company. Ask them to come to the meeting with a list of things they want to talk about. When you ask what they want from you, don't get upset if some answer "more money." Specialist retailing is not a hobby. We all want a better life. (Wasn't "How much money do you want to make?" one of your job interview questions, anyway?)

You may be surprised at what people consider "better," though. For some, a "better job" means different days off or more training. Back-office staff want to become salespeople, and salespeople want to become owners. The big-box stores aren't small enough to accommodate such individual needs. You are. You *can* make your store the place your employees want to work for the rest of their careers.

Then again, an employee might tell you she wants to start her own business. If you feel she can pull it off, you may want to have a partner in a new store rather than a competitor. The point is, you can never know what your people have on their minds until you ask.

TIP #5. Make the meeting a pleasant one.

Do everything you can to make your employees comfortable at the performance interview. Bring in coffee cake or something special. Remember: You're the team leader, not the parole board. If you think this sounds a little too cozy, well... why shouldn't it? Haven't we said one of the benefits of independent retailers is that they are small enough that long-time co-workers come to feel like family?

The only unexpected news you deliver to employees at these reviews should be of a positive nature, so go out of your way to make it a mutually beneficial, low-stress meeting. After all, having taken charge of your store with progressive discipline, all the bad news should already be out in the open.

Taking charge also implies that such interviews take place on a regular basis — every six months, if possible. And the more you review your employees, the more you're taking charge of your store's success.

At Chicago Brass, C.J. holds 54 performance review sessions a year: Every Friday, he buys the entire crew breakfast, and they discuss their wants and needs — a free exchange of kudos and criticism over coffee. (C.J. also conducts private, written reviews every six months.) If you think weekly reviews are a little excessive, let me introduce you to the owner of Richard's Music in Jackson, Mississippi. Richard Kubow reviews his people each and every day.

> Bring in coffee cake or something special. You're the team leader, not the parole board.

Specialist Spotlight on

Richard's Music

ife as a retail manager was never on piano man Richard Kubow's playlist. He'd even be the first to tell you that, as a musician, he's part of a class of people who can't even manage themselves, let alone others. A man's upbringing has a way of catching up with him, though. "There's no way my mom was going to let me become a musician," he laughs. "A musician's future is much too uncertain, so I got a degree in business instead."

Richard wasn't quite ready for life in a pin-striped suit, though. Soon after his 1975 graduation, he moved from his safe haven in Decatur, Illinois, to the poorest part of Jackson, Mississippi, and joined the civil rights movement at the Voice of Calvary Ministries. But it wasn't long before he discovered that the missionary business is non-profit to the point of non-payment. Supplementing his nearly non-existent paycheck became a priority. He figured having a degree in business would at least qualify him to, well… give music lessons. So in his spare time he taught piano at an acoustic guitar shop.

But times, they were a'changin', and the owner of the little acoustic guitar store just couldn't keep up. More "Afro-Americans" were moving into the neighborhood, and black folks bought pianos, electric basses, and keyboards, not acoustic guitars. His business no longer fit in, so he decided to close up shop.

Richard realized that the only way to save his job was to buy the store. So in 1981, he arranged with the owner to buy the place the same way he'd purchased his car: one month at a time. That was more than 260 months ago. He now owns the company lock, stock, and musical barrel.

Already entrenched in the black community, the fledgling entrepreneur was in tune with its needs. He knew that the folks in his neighborhood traditionally played by ear, largely because few had access to formal lessons. Although the community was now doing much better economically, the tradition remained.

So why not develop a method for teaching piano by ear, Richard thought. If that's what the community wants, he might as well give it to them. He had unwittingly stumbled onto an idea that would eventually make him a genuine specialist. Richard invented the first "play by ear" piano method — and the music he taught his customers was Gospel.

The neighborhood went nuts. They flocked to Richard's Music by the carload. Every R&B artist in town played in church on Sunday — and Richard's Music was soon known as *the* place to learn how to play. Eventually he moved the store to a new location, right between the black and white communities, and began teaching "white Gospel" as well as black. As his customer base doubled and business skyrocketed, so did the number of people he employed.

Now, because Richard's Music is just down the street from Morrison's Brothers Music, one of the country's largest music retailers, he has a hard time making a profit on instruments. Combine that challenge with the competition he faces today from catalog sales and the Internet, and you can see that Richard's market is a tough one indeed.

Fortunately, music lessons represented the one arena in which the big guys could not compete. Although only 20% or so of his store's income came from teaching, it represented a huge profit category.

Yet teaching turned out to be a double-edged sword. It was profitable, but the teachers themselves turned out to be a true management nightmare. Almost without exception, every teacher Richard hired seemed to

> Music lessons represented the one arena in which the big guys could not compete.

view his policy manual as *The Piano Man's Big Book of Suggestions*, rather than actual rules for running a business. He actually endured one 22-month period during which he hired and fired 18 teachers.

With turnover representing the store's largest expense, Richard decided it was time for a little reflection. There must have been some good teachers in the batch, so what went wrong? He decided the failing must be his.

All he expected was that they follow a few rules, complete a little paperwork, and come in on time. They refused. The reason seemed obvious to Richard. The secret to managing them better was not.

"They're musicians," he said. "They're all right-brainers. The only thing they use the left hemisphere of their brains for is their equipment — picks and cables and stuff. I don't know if they refuse to do paperwork, or they just can't! It makes no difference to me. It's part of the job. I salary my teachers. I pay each one enough to raise a family. Yet they would rather work someplace else for less than do the six minutes of paperwork required out of every hour."

Then one morning a few years back, Richard recalled an article he'd once read about the early manned Moon flights. The author had noted that those early Moon rocketships were off course about 90% of their time in flight —- but that every so often the astronauts fired little retro-rockets for a couple of seconds to get the ship back on course. The men were not blaming their Moon-bound vehicles for being off course. All they were doing was giving them a little extra direction.

Richard thought about his workers. "They're grownups," he mused. "They don't need reprimands. They need course correction. They need some retro-rockets!"

Since his turnover was astronomical anyway, he didn't worry about the current staff bailing on him. What difference could it make at this stage?

So he instituted daily "course corrections" for his staff. Here's how they work: Every day at 2:00 p.m., Richard leaves his wife (also the store's bookkeeper) in charge while he meets for an hour with his salespeople and teachers to distribute and review his "retro-rocket reports." The employees learn precisely what they did right and what they did wrong the preceding day. That's right, Richard writes them up everyday in front of the entire staff.

He is quick to note that he's not talking about major rule infractions. A question of theft or a problem that requires a serious reprimand, if not dismissal, would be handled in private, of course.

The daily "course corrections" address the details of store procedure. "Mike, you forgot to put down on the appointment schedule that next week is Bobby Smith's fourth lesson. If you're not here next week for some reason, the substitute won't know Bobby's expected skill level." The employee signs the retro-rocket form — and you can bet he's careful not to look like a knucklehead in front of his co-workers by repeating the same mistake.

If Mike's problem becomes chronic, chances are the other employees will straighten him out. They know Mike is going to get fired if he doesn't get back on course, and they don't want that to happen. It's bad for the team. Richard says he's rarely forced to write an official reprimand for his employees' files. They usually quit first.

How did his original team adapt to the change when he launched the retro-rocket scheme back in 2001? With a single exception, every one of

> The daily "course corrections" address the details of store procedure.

them eventually quit, much as he had expected. The replacement team knows no other way, accepting the daily meetings as just part of the job. If new recruits take issue with the practice, the others even assure them it's cool.

Richard says no one seems to mind that the review process doesn't take place in private. By keeping everything out in the open, it's clear no one is getting special treatment. And for anyone who might have too few brain cells left to remember the rules, the mini-evaluations are a great reminder of precisely the behavior the boss expects.

Everyone still makes mistakes — and every employee is written up every single day. But they all know that their team and the store are better for it. After all, how many of their superstore competitors have time for such daily improvement sessions? One of his teachers was late the other day and even wrote herself up, handing Richard the paperwork to sign. Talk about instilling a sense of responsibility in your employees!

Thanks to his daily "course corrections," Richard doesn't need to conduct formal employee reviews like other businesses. "A baseball player doesn't need a quarterly review," he says, switching gears from space- to sports-related metaphors. "He gets his review every time he goes to the plate. If he gets sent to the minors, it's a surprise to no one. He gets real-time feedback every time he suits up. That's what I give my people: instant feedback. Feedback truly is the breakfast of champions. And right now, I have myself a championship team."

S ome stores have more of a problem with theft than others. Chicago Brass Decorative Plumbing and Hardware is one of those specialist stores fortunate to have very little theft. "There's no aftermarket for what we sell," says owner C.J. Schnakenberg, whom you met back on Page 38. "You can't really stand on the corner in a trench coat, open it to a passerby, and say, 'Hey buddy, you wanna buy a faucet?'"

Sadly, most retailers aren't so lucky. And specialist retailers are in a particularly difficult category: Because of the smaller size and more intimate atmosphere of independent stores, it's easy to come to feel as if your people are family. And none of us likes to think of our family members as potential thieves.

It's not uncommon for managers to have a clear-eyed view of the potential for shoplifting at their stores — and to take steps to combat it — while wearing blinders to the potential for theft from the people they trust the most. Yet, in my experience, *your own employees* are to blame for more than half of the shoplifting at *your store.*

Now, I'm the least cynical person in the world... but I've been taken advantage of so many times that I've had to become a store cop. Assume that everyone will steal from you, take preemptive action, and you'll never be disappointed.

Assuming everyone will steal is not the same as treating your employees like potential thieves, however! Let's get that clear up front. It means taking charge of your valuables in a way that will minimize the opportunities for theft — *and* allow you to spot it as soon as it occurs. Leave a batch of chocolate chip cookies cooling on the counter when the kids come home and, sure enough, they'll be out to steal them from

Chapter 8
To Catch a Thief

the start. Lock 'em up (I mean the cookies...), and you needn't spend the rest of the day hunting for a tell-tale trail of crumbs.

Before discussing how to stop employee theft, I want you to consider *why* and *how* it occurs. Imagine a three-point triangle (as opposed to a four-point triangle, which would be a square). Let's call this our "theft triangle" — the situation in which all factors necessary for employee theft are present.

The first point on our imaginary triangle is *desire*. If your employees do not want either your merchandise or your cash, they will not steal. Unfortunately, in this regard, many of your workers were probably drawn to your store because they *love* what you sell. They are audiophiles and bibliophiles, model train fanatics and car stereo buffs, hobbyists and aficionados of every shape and size. What makes such people *ideal* employees — their passion for your products — is the very thing that can work against you when it comes to employee theft.

The second point on our triangle is *ability*, specifically a person's moral ability to perform a dishonest act. Say that 10% of your employees are truly dishonest people — but another 80% could steal if sorely tempted. As I said, I'm not a cynic, but....

The last point on our triangle is *opportunity*. If you carry products that your employees desire, and you hire people who are morally capable of stealing, *they will steal if given the opportunity*. But remove the opportunity, and you can control your losses. Think back to Di-No Computers, the computer store profiled in *Thriving in the Shadow of Giants*.[3] Owner Sal Cordaro has removed the opportunity for employee theft at his store by

---

[3] *Thriving in the Shadow of Giants: How to Find Success as an Independent Retailer* by Eddy Kay. Book I in the GOOD NEWS ABOUT RETAILING series. Available at www.goodnewsabout.com.

hiring a clerk responsible only for shipping, receiving, and inventory. This individual now conducts continual inventory checks of high-theft items like software and inspects every box shipped out to customers.

In addition, Sal took trash removal off the employee responsibility list after finding merchandise in trash bags in the dumpster — an all-too-common method of employee theft. The maintenance company now removes all trash from the store. The deterrence has worked: Sal now boasts a zero theft rate.

Eliminating one or more of the three points on our theft triangle will help you put a stop to employee theft. Since you can't control your employees' moral make-up, the most you can do is try to screen out the blatantly dishonest applicants before you even hire them. And since most specialists *want* staff members with a passion for their products, it turns out the only point on our triangle you actually have any hope of controlling is opportunity.

How do we minimize the opportunities for internal theft then? Well, I have a few ideas to start you off. Even if the following tips appear elementary, please don't skip ahead! Say you already have a front-door policy, or you've told your salespeople that random cash drawer audits will be conducted, are you actually doing these things? And is every manager — and the owner, too — required to follow these security procedures, or just the staff?

TIP #1. Control entrance and exit points.

The back, or side, door is the thief's exit at most stores. No employee should enter or leave by a back or side door — and that includes the owner and managers. *You* must take charge by setting a good example.

> No employee should enter or leave by a back or side door — and that includes the owner and managers.

If the back or side door needs to be opened to receive shipments, the owner or a manager should monitor the transaction, then secure the door immediately afterward.

"But Eddy," you might ask, "I have a car stereo store, or some other type of retail outfit that requires work-bay doors. I don't have to make my guys in the back go through the store to leave, do I?" It doesn't matter what your store's layout is. The front-door rule must hold. I understand your people will resist (and believe in their hearts that you've lost your mind) when you announce that everyone must traipse through the showroom every time they leave. That's okay.

Point out that when they own their own store, they can run it any old way they want. Then explain the *whys* of your new rule, and they'll come around: Uncontrolled exit points lead to employee theft... and employee theft leads to a weak bottom line... and a weak bottom line leads to less money for raises and employee benefits. Now you're speaking their language!

TIP #2. Lock down your inventory.

When you look around your store, you shouldn't see any merchandise at all. You should see stacks and stacks of $100 bills piled on those shelves. It's amazing how many specialist retailers have an "oh well" attitude about their missing wares. Cashmere sweater missing from the stack? "Hmmm, oh well." Bike pump missing from the display? "Hmmm, oh well." Building missing from the lot? "Hmmmmmm... oh well!" Theft is part of the cost of doing business, isn't it? *No, it's not!*

As much merchandise as is feasible should be locked up in a stockroom or cage. Now obviously, what is "feasible" varies from industry to industry. Camera specialists can and should have most of their merchandise locked up in displays. Don't $800 lenses look even better reflecting off gleaming glass and chrome anyway? Conversely, the mystery bookstore owner will want to keep most of her books out on attractive shelves that encourage browsing — except those signed first editions of Elmore Leonard's *Forty Lashes Less One*, of course.

One person (usually the owner or a manager, and both should be watching each other) should have access to whatever inventory you've determined can be secured behind lock and key. And that person must be accountable for it!

If a salesperson asks for an expensive piece of merchandise out of inventory to show a customer, that inventory control person should be keeping track of what happens to that item until it is returned to the shelf. Depending on your market, a sign-out log of merchandise given to employees for customer demonstrations is not a bad idea either.

I once walked into one of the 22 stores I was managing and passed the manager leaving with a brand-new radio tucked under his arm.

"Where are you going with that?" I enquired.

"Oh, this is for my cousin," he replied. "He'll give me the money tonight, and tomorrow I'll write it up."

"Are you nuts?!" I asked. "Nothing goes out of here without a paid invoice!" The man looked at me as if I had just kicked his dog.

I ordered an audit of the store the next day. Guess what I found? Perhaps the better question is: Guess what I didn't?

> I ordered an audit of the store the next day. Guess what I found? Perhaps the better question is: Guess what I didn't?

You won't always catch the merchandise in someone's hands, of course. Merchandise left on a back table for several days for no apparent reason is almost certainly destined for someone's trunk.

TIP #3. Count your inventory on a regular basis — and let your employees help.

At least once a month, a manager and team of employees should undertake a complete and detailed inventory. You want to verify that what you expect to be on your shelves and in the stockroom actually is there. Take smaller "cycle counts" daily on key areas. Pick a single vendor or a small category for these daily audits.

These cycle counts serve two purposes. First, if there is any merchandise missing, it's easier to remember where to find something you just lost yesterday than to try tracking it down after a regular inventory a month later.

Second, and perhaps more important, is the deterrent effect of such regular inventory checks. Cycle counts alert your employees that you care about where your merchandise is. If they know that any errant items will be investigated quickly, they're less likely to risk stealing.

TIP #4. Schedule return handling.

Establish a separate area in your stockroom for manufacturer returns, and then process all merchandise held in this area at a specific time each week. Require your staff to use a standard form for every single return or exchange and to attach a copy of the sales receipt to the form at the time it is filled out. (In some industries, manufacturers require that the sales receipt for a defective item be returned to them.) A set location for returned items, and set procedures for handling them, will eliminate the opportunities for your wares to slip through the cracks.

TIP #5. Start controlling your cash.

Seriously! Get a cash register if you don't have one, and assign one person to work it. I kid you not when I say that there are still mom-and-pops out there making change out of cigar boxes. And they keep those boxes right under their credit card machines. If the owner, the manager, the entire sales team, *and* the stock boy all have their hands in the cash register, how can you possibly account for any lost money? If only one person handles the drawer, you know where to point the finger when a problem arises.

Then, balance your cash daily. Don't keep a floating drawer for days at a time. Start with a fixed bank (say $100) that is verified by the employee assigned to the cash drawer. At the end of the day, don't total up your invoices and take that amount from the register. Instead, count the $100 bank for the next day and compare the money that you have left against the invoices written for the day. That way you will see the actual overages or shortages for the day.

Next, spot-check the register several times a week. Count the bank in the middle of the day without warning, and compare the remainder against invoices. It should only take a few minutes to do this. (Just don't start the process when you have 10 customers in line waiting to pay. We all know how annoying it is when managers do that in the fast lane at the supermarket.)

At the end of the day, compare the overages/shortages against your earlier audit. If the drawer is short, you can pinpoint the time of day

> If only one person handles the drawer, you know where to point the finger when a problem arises.

(either before or after the audit) the shortage occurred. Sure, we all make mistakes. But repeated shortages are a big red flag that you have a problem somewhere.

However, repeated shortages in mid-day audits that *disappear* by the end of the day should also send that red flag sky-high. They are a good indication that someone is stealing money and then fudging the paperwork afterward to balance out the shortage.

On a related note, paper clips, matches, or loose coins found in or around your cash registers are other clues that this type of theft is happening. Employees will use such items as markers to remember how much money has been removed, and thus know how much fudging needs to be done.

Lastly, require that a manager handle all sales to friends or family of employees if you offer a staff discount (see Tip #7). Hired hands often believe you can afford to take a loss every so often. You do not want these people deciding what you can and cannot afford. Many of them have 28 brothers and sisters. Well, I want to see the birth certificates.

TIP #6. Establish a petty-cash fund.

All businesses need money from time to time for postage, office supplies, or other minor (but immediate) needs. The cash for such expenses should never, ever come from your registers. And get rid of that cigar box in your right-hand desk drawer. Everyone knows it's there. Instead, maintain a petty-cash fund in a lockbox, locked drawer, or safe to keep these costs separate from your sales. The total of the remaining cash and the receipts in your petty-cash fund should *always* total the amount originally set up for the fund.

Not only will a petty-cash fund help your accountant keep things straight, it keeps employees out of the cash register for anything but handling sales. A question about missing money can never turn into, "Oh yeah, I forgot that I paid the delivery guy last week. Sorry, I didn't get a receipt."

TIP #7. Offer a generous employee discount.

By offering to sell your wares at cost, and allowing employees and their immediate family members to take full advantage of manufacturer discounts, you're giving those who would be tempted less reason to steal from you. And even if every person on your team is as honest as a blind man in an art gallery, a substantial employee discount is a nice perk for all the rest of your honest, hard-working team members.

TIP #8. Loan 'em money if they need it.

One successful drugstore company I know has a policy that allows employees to ask the store manager for a small pocket-cash loan. The limit is $20 and must be paid back on the next payday. Managers even encourage employees to take advantage of the policy. Why? If they freely loan the cash, the need to steal when an employee's stomach begins to growl or the gas tank is on zero is greatly reduced.

TIP #9. Love the people who work for you!

Well, appreciate them and treat them fairly, at least. Most employees caught stealing say they did so because they were "owed" the money or merchandise for some workplace injustice. Besides, they don't feel their stealing hurt anybody, because they were stealing from "the business." By providing a good work atmosphere, by being strict with your rules

> Most employees caught stealing say they did so because they were "owed" the money for some workplace injustice.

but friendly with your people, by praising your employees' accomplishments and supporting them when they fail but want to learn, you'll make it much less likely that your people will want to steal from you.

After all, the notion that "employees are family" — an attitude that independent retailers are small enough to enjoy — works both ways.

TIP #10. Set a good example.

What applies to your employees applies to you, too! Follow your own rules to the letter, and make sure everyone sees that you are following them. Above all, be honest in all of your dealings. If a vendor sends you duplicate orders without charging you, don't put the extras on your shelf. "Hey, everyone!" you should say. "We got an extra sweater from Pendleton. Billy, do me a favor. Call them up and let them know so we can ship it back. I'm sure they'll appreciate our honesty."

Karma, kismet, heaven, or hell. What goes around, comes around. Honest employers attract honest employees. Dishonest ones, well…?

TIP #11. If you catch a thief, play hardball.

It's a sad day when you catch someone red-handed. When it happens, many managers simply tell the individual to leave and never return. The problem is that such a dismissal sends a "no big deal" lesson to the other employees, some of whom may also be stealing. There's no better message that you are serious than to have a thief walk out of the store in handcuffs.

We all know that measures like installing security cameras or conducting background checks will help prevent employee theft. The common denominator in these 11 suggestions is that they cost you nothing. (Well, unless you really *are* running your store without a cash register or a few secure display cases.) Any specialist retailer could implement such changes in policy and procedure tomorrow. They represent simple ways to take charge of your store by attacking your problem, not your people. And the good news is that you don't have to be the bad guy — *if* you apply these rules universally and consistently, as the family team featured in our next SPECIALIST SPOTLIGHT has learned.

You don't have to be the bad guy if you apply these rules universally and consistently.

Specialist Spotlight on

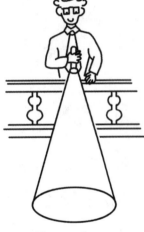

Breakers Mobile Electronics

B reaker, one-nine, breaker, one-nine. Come in, good buddy. This is the Motor City Rambler looking for some motion lotion on the flip-flop from LA-LA-Land." Laugh today, but back in the 1970s those words were no joke. Those coded phrases represented big money… and the telephone call that would eventually make Robert Graham, president of Breakers Mobile Electronics in Oxnard, California, the success he is today.

Bob's always been a hustler when it comes to making a living. I guess anyone growing up near the metropolis of Waterloo, Iowa, has to think creatively in order to make any money. That goes double if you're 18 and just out of high school. In the early 1970s, Bob and a friend came up with a clever business idea.

In the days before the big-box retailers, people bought their televisions at the local mom-and-pop appliance store. When folks wanted a new TV, they just brought in the old one for a trade. Now, Mom and Pop had no use for those used TVs (other than to justify the discount they'd just given you). So they sold them to Bob and Co. for $10 or $15. These entrepreneurial guys would repair the TVs, polish up the boxes, and resell them for $200. What a country!

Enter the VCR in the late 1970s, and with it a shift from appliance outlets to specialty stores as the retailer of choice for TVs. Bob was running out of used inventory. Knowing he had no choice but to adapt to the changing times, Bob headed to sunny Southern California and began selling cars until he could find his way.

Back in Iowa, Bob's brother-in-law was going gangbusters as a CB radio distributor. Talking to the folks back home one day, Bob learned that his brother-in-law was willing to sell him as many of the radios at wholesale as he wanted. Amusingly enough, Bob didn't even know what a CB was, but he headed back to Iowa to find out. "In 14 days, I did a 180," he says, "learning all about CBs, the accessories, and how to promote them."

Back in California, he started selling this hot new product out of his own house. In characteristic Bob style, he threw himself wholeheartedly into his newfound business, even starting a CB club.

Pretty soon he had just about as much business as he could handle… and definitely more than his neighbors were willing to tolerate. He was forced to find a retail location. What did he name the new store? "Breaker 1-9."

By the early 1980s, the public was losing its fascination with CBs just as car stereo was coming into vogue. Ever the early adopter, Bob began to buy mobile hi-fi from the same distributors who sold him CBs. It wasn't long before CB radios had become such a niche market that Bob decided to get out of the business altogether.

Since his Oxnard store was only blocks from the Pacific Ocean, he decided to change its name. He dropped the one-nine, put waves on both sides, and christened the place Breakers Mobile Electronics.

Twenty-some years later, Breakers is still making waves. As his general manager of sales, Bob's daughter Bobbi Grantham runs the place like a pro. Her husband, Steve, joined the pop-and-daughter operation as Breakers' general manager of service. And Bob himself is now a well-known industry figure. Past president of the Mobile Enhancement Retailers Association, he credits his success to smart management as well as an entrepreneurial spirit.

> Ever the early adopter, Bob began to buy mobile hi-fi from the same distributors who sold him CBs.

Over the years, Bob has learned that a passion for the products you sell and a willingness to change with the times aren't always enough.

"It takes a serious commitment to training to get your salespeople to be able to lead your customers through the process of the sale," he says. At least training can be fun. "Putting controls on your employees is less of a pleasant task for management," he adds.

Employee theft is one of the greatest challenges for retailers in the mobile electronics industry. Perhaps even more so than in many other markets, car stereo specialists attract hobbyists, which means that the desire point of our theft triangle is even more prominent in this industry than in others.

Add to that not-so-good news the fact that car stereo products are not cheap — *and* are easily resold at flea markets or out of a trunk, no questions asked — and it's easy to see how employee theft can, and does, put such stores out of business.

Bob has managed to keep his head well above water with a two-fold approach. First, he eliminates temptation by eliminating access. Only a fraction of the Breakers team has warehouse access — and among that fraction, Bob counts Bobbi, who's worked there since she was 13, and her husband, who's worked there since he was 14.

Second, Bob keeps his inventory under tight control… by turning it a whopping 24 times a year. Yes, it's true! Most retailers would be thrilled with four turns a year, meaning you've sold out of everything you have four times in 12 months. Bob orders merchandise every single week. With the good fortune of having most of his suppliers within a 100-mile radius of the store, Bob's money is never tied up in boxes.

"I can't believe these guys who do $2 million a year in business and have half a million in inventory," he says. "What do they do when business slows down?" Breakers had a six-month slow period last year, but Bob never missed a single payment — and never lost his "quick pay" discount with his vendors either. What cash he had was still flowing.

When you turn your inventory as often as they do at Breakers, it's easy to spot missing merchandise. If you had three Cool Dude Subwoofer boxes on the warehouse shelf yesterday, and suddenly there's a big empty space, you've either made a good sale or lost valuable stock.

In addition to keeping daily tabs on inventory, Bob watches out for what he calls "bad indicators" in his employees. The person who comes in unshaved on a regular basis, or is consistently late for work, represents a high-risk for theft in Bob's view. So is the one who's always complaining about the company and exhibits a poor response to the twice-yearly employee interviews.

Heading high-risk employees off before they even join your team is the key, of course. Bob initiated drug screening for applicants back in 1999 after hearing from colleagues in his retailers association that the tactic had been a good deterrent for problem employees at their stores.

Still, thieves slip through. "Catching them and proving your case is very tough," says Bob. "The thief usually catches on or quits before we can do anything."

Although he's never caught anyone walking out the door with merchandise under his arm, Bob has had to call the police after employees have left under suspicious circumstances. "They've come down to take a report," he says, "but they just call it an 'internal problem.'" But such

When you turn your inventory as often as they do at Breakers, it's easy to spot missing merchandise.

investigations are "quite extensive," he adds, "and it upsets the entire store." The police end up questioning all of the employees — an indication that the theft is no little matter... and perhaps a good deterrent to anyone else contemplating a similar crime.

The occasional problem aside, Bob's hands-on approach to eliminating employee theft means that he's been able to assemble the best retail team around. Sure, Southern California is rife with superstore competitors, but Bob's not worried.

"My salespeople are what separate us from the big guys," he says. "My people are professionals. They follow up on leads, call people back, don't give everything away, and feel good about what they do for a living. The big-box salespeople are usually there because they couldn't find jobs doing anything else."

10-four, good buddy.

Congratulations, you're ready to take charge of your store! You've learned how to hire, inspire, and sometimes fire your employees… how to use the Show Me game to teach them *The World According to You*… how to address issues like internal theft by attacking the problem, not the people… and how to stand up to the superstores by standing out from the crowd — by offering the kind of good, old-fashioned customer service that never goes out of style.

You've also learned that, if you've been finding life as a manager stressful, the problem is a lack of control. Think about what exactly stress is. I like to define it as "pressure without control." I may be under pressure to make my mortgage payment, but I don't feel any stress because I am secure in my job. I know the bills will get paid. But if I lose my job and can't find another? I have no control over the means to handle the pressure of my mortgage. Now we're talking *stress.*

Managing an independent retail store is no different. The pressure to succeed… to boost your bottom line, to increase your customer base, to thrive in the shadow of those big-box retail giants… is always with you. But if you have no control over the *means* to achieve that success — your employees — your life will be filled with nothing but stress. Take charge, and the stress goes away!

Please don't misunderstand me, though: Pressure itself is not a bad thing. Pressure is *good.* It gets the job done. And, sometimes, it can make getting the job done a lot more fun.

I remember a particular sales contest among the managers back when I was running a shop in an 18-store chain. First prize? A free weekend in San Diego for the entire family. (Second through 18th places would

Chapter 9
Good News About Retailing!

receive the ridicule of the first.) As we neared the finish line, I was neck and neck for the winning spot. I'd call my rival at the end of each day and ask what he "had out." He'd give me the number, which I would immediately divide by my age.

During the last few days of that contest, I couldn't even sleep, I was so busy preparing mentally for the following day's battle. It was fun. In fact, it was the pressure that made it a blast.

Fast forward a few years... and there I was, preparing to speak to a large audience at a *Fortune* 500 company. The attendees were seated. I was introduced. I pushed the button on my remote control to bring up the first slide in my PowerPoint show. The computer shut itself off. The thing was as dead as my acting career. A sea of blank faces wavered in front of me, heartlessly oblivious to my predicament.

I was about to give a seminar with no slides, no props, and no show business. I had to rely on talent. With no control over the situation, and under pressure to deliver a magnificent show, I had a headache the size of small-block Chevy V8 (with a stomach to match) 30 seconds later.

Stress *hurts.*

So, stop reading for a moment, and try my little test for how much stress potential you still have: take a look at your key ring. I've always believed that the true sign of a successful adult is his number of keys. The proper number, of course, being two: one for the house and one for the car.

It seems that the more things and places you have to lock up and keep track of, the less time you have for yourself. But, now that you've taken charge, you can start getting rid of some of those keys!

Back in my days managing a 22-store chain, I had little time for me… and 37 pounds of keys. There's no discrete place to put so many keys. In my back pocket, they were a pain in the butt. In my front pocket, people thought I was bragging. On my belt, they not only clashed with my Façonnable suit, people thought I was stealing silverware.

Other annoying little things made it clear to me that I was definitely not in control in those days. The security company had me as the first person to call no matter which store had an alarm go off — despite the fact that I had a manager who literally lived down the street from one of our locations. This guy never missed a night's sleep. He knew I would always answer the telephone, so he didn't.

One evening, while my manager was getting his beauty rest, my phone rang. It was the cops.

"Mr. Kay?"

"Yes."

"This is the Covina police department calling."

"How nice of you to call. I like getting up four or five hours before work. It gives me a chance to brush my teeth and grab a cup of coffee."

"Sir, it seems your store is open."

Open? Did the manager forget to lock up? Did the wind rattle the door?

"What do you mean by open? Do you mean unlocked?" (Maybe I could take care of things in the morning....)

> Other annoying little things made it clear to me that I was definitely not in control in those days.

"Sir, the store is open — and you should come down here."

"Can you give me any more information? Is anything wrong other than the alarm going off?"

"Sir, the store is open — and you should come down here."

Fine, don't tell me. I'll drag myself out of bed and drive over to the store. The same store run by a manager sleeping two blocks away.

I arrived at a scene that resembled a close encounter of the worst kind. Radios squawking, red lights flashing, bulletproof-vested officers crawling over patrol cars... The store was indeed "open." In fact, the front of the building was completely missing. Someone had backed a truck through it.

The police asked for my identification. When they were satisfied I was management, they loaded themselves and their fancy gear into their patrol cars and drove away. There I stood, alone in a parking lot covered with a thousand square feet of broken glass, timber, and trash. I felt as helpless as a child — and definitely *not* in control... of the situation, of my job, of my stores, or of my life.

Was I supposed to protect what's left of the store with my Swiss Army Knife? Let's see, do I have that special blade that puts buildings back together? Nope, wrong model.

Staring at a building that might have been transported to Southern California from the wrong part of Baghdad, I realized that I couldn't just leave (the pressure of responsibility), but I had no idea how to fix the situation (no control). I was stressed to the max.

Because I changed managers as often as my socks, I *had* to be on the security call list in those days — a fact this one helpful manager was quick to realize. And he was just one of 22 managers under me. What about the rest of the staff?! I had all these salespeople, each with their own agenda, story, and excuses for why they simply could not do what I expected them to.

So, if that's how you were feeling when you picked up this book, it's okay. You're *not* alone! It only seems that way sometimes. Thousands of managers of independent specialist stores just like yours enjoy fulfilling, stress-free jobs. You've met some of them in the SPOTLIGHTS throughout this book. Sam Sr. and his sons at Best Brands Plus, Elizabeth and Josie at Flying Pig Children's Books... These folks can't wait to go to work every day, because work is fun. Their employees follow the rules, and their customers just keep coming back. Life is good.

The good news — no, *great* news! — is that successful retailers such as these nice folks are really no smarter or more talented than you. They just have a little more information, and a few more tools, than you did before you started reading this book. Do what you've always done... and you'll get what you've always gotten. Take charge... and you'll get what you've always wanted.

By the way... the family had a great time in San Diego.

> Thousands of managers of independent specialist stores just like yours enjoy fulfilling, stress-free jobs.

Specialist Spotlight on

Goldfish Plus

As a fish-ianado since childhood, Peter Pang knows pretty much everything there is to know about fish. So, after retiring as director of sales and training for Van de Kamp Bakery in the early 1990s, he decided to go fishing... for customers, that is. In 1992, Peter opened up Goldfish Plus, purveyors of fine fish and reptiles, in Covina, California.

As the principal in his school of seven staffers, Peter has the final say on every transaction and rings up every sale. As his employees swim from customer to customer, he hovers in the background, answering questions and recommending products. He goes to great lengths to ensure that his customers — *and* his merchandise — can look forward to a long and happy life together.

Mr. Moneybags could walk into Goldfish Plus with tufts of hundred-dollar bills falling from his pockets and declare that he'll buy every fish on the spot. But he won't get far until he brings in a water sample.

A *what?*

Peter won't touch a scale on his critters' heads unless he knows that the customer has a good home for his prospective pet. Besides, in a business where client relations are crucial, a Kissing Gourami floating belly-up in Junior's aquarium is not the best business card to be leaving behind. Avoiding such mishaps means conducting a chemical analysis of the water the fish will call home.

Don't have the right tank? Water's not quite right? Peter will sell you everything you need. Goldfish Plus carries a wide variety of merchandise, some made just for the store, and Peter will special-order whatever he doesn't have in stock.

His staff will install it, too. This is where things get really interesting. Four of Peter's seven employees keep a personal trade of customer accounts for whom they do home servicing. If customer X has a problem with a leaky tank, or the Dalmatian Molly's swimming at an odd list, staffer Y will always be the one to take care of it.

And his employees love this home service so much that Peter doesn't even have to pay them to do the work. The customers do that. Staffers who go out on a call are off the clock — but they keep the entire fee the store charges for the house call. This is much better than working for scale. (Oh my cod, did I really say that?) After years of working at Goldfish Plus and compiling a huge list of customer contacts, one of Peter's employees doesn't even work in the store anymore. As a college student, he no longer has the time. But he still makes house calls.

Talk about a pay structure that works! The benefits of such a creative arrangement are obvious: Peter's customers get unprecedented levels of service, he pays little for it (his insurance policy does cover the workers on such calls), and his employees haul in the catch. This is no fish story!

Some of Peter's customers come from as much as 100 miles away. With that kind of client base, it's easy to see why he doesn't worry about the competition. There may be bigger fish in the sea, but none of them knows as much about their products as the team at Goldfish Plus does.

One competitor actually closed its fish department six months after Goldfish Plus opened its doors, and the local PETCO and PETSMART locations refer customers to Peter's store on a regular basis. "We are a little thing compared to the giant stores," he says, "but we get a lot of respect from our competitors." The big guys obviously know that, when it comes to fish, at Goldfish Plus there's no sea-horsin' around.

> His employees love this home service so much that Peter doesn't even have to pay them to do the work.

Appendix A
The Good News Reading List

ACCOUNTING AND FINANCE

BURTON, E. JAMES AND STEVEN M. BRAGG. *Accounting and Finance for Your Small Business*. John Wiley and Sons Inc. (2000). Includes forms, checklists, and other tools for analyzing key information, as well as real-world examples showing practical applications.

FRIEDLOB, GEORGE THOMAS. *Financial and Business Statements*. Barron's Educational Series (2000). Emphasis is on daily operations, with descriptions of how to use P&Ls, balance sheets, and other basic business and accounting statements.

EMPLOYEE THEFT

BRYANT, BARRY. *101 + Ways to Steal... By a Cashier*. Wash Davis Corp. (1999). Bryant interviewed hundreds of thieves to document theft by employees, vendors, customers, and robbers and offers suggestions for dealing with theft before it costs you your business.

JENNINGS, RON AND JACKIE JENNINGS. *Employee Theft: How to Spot It, How to Stop It!*. Business Owners Press (1994). How to limit opportunities for internal theft by controlling your accounting.

INTERVIEWS, REVIEWS, AND EMPLOYEE HANDBOOKS

DEBLIEUX, MIKE. *Performance Appraisal Source Book: A Collection of Practical Examples*. Society for Human Resource Management (2003). The book includes a CD-ROM and 40 sample forms for a variety of performance review situations.

DOUGLAS, MAX AND ROBERT BACAL. *Perfect Phrases for Performance Reviews: Hundreds of Ready-to-Use Phrases That Describe Your Employees' Performance*. McGraw-Hill Trade (2002). Help for those daunted by the prospect of making just the "right comments" on employee performance reviews.

FALCONE, PAUL. *96 Great Interview Questions to Ask Before You Hire.* AMACOM (1997). A guide to identifying high-performance job candidates and spotting "red flags" that indicate evasions or lies.

FALCONE, PAUL. *101 Sample Write-Ups for Documenting Employee Performance Problems.* AMACOM (1999). Ready-to-use sample forms cover every imaginable disciplinary problem.

FEIN, RICHARD. *101 Hiring Mistakes Employers Make... and How to Avoid Them.* Impact Publications (2000). A useful guide for retailers preparing to reassess their hiring practices.

GUERIN, LISA AND AMY DELPO. *Create Your Own Employee Handbook: A Legal and Practical Guide.* Nolo Press (2003). A step-by-step guide to (almost) painlessly putting together your own employee manual, available at www.nolo.com.

GUERIN, LISA AND AMY DELPO. *Dealing With Problem Employees: A Legal Guide.* Nolo Press (2003). More great advice from Nolo authors Guerin and DelPo, available at www.nolo.com.

SUPERSTORE COMPETITION

KAY, EDDY. *Raking in the Dough: Real-World Advice for Making a Sales Career in Specialty Retailing.* GOOD NEWS ABOUT RETAILING Book III (Winter 2003). Available at www.goodnewsabout.com.

KAY, EDDY. *Thriving in the Shadow of Giants: How to Find Success as an Independent Retailer.* GOOD NEWS ABOUT RETAILING Book I (2002). Available at www.goodnewsabout.com.

TAYLOR, DON AND JEANNE SMALLING ARCHER. *Up Against the Wal-Marts.* AMACOM (1996). You *can* compete with the superstores.

STONE, KENNETH E. *Competing with the Retail Giants.* John Wiley & Sons (1995). Excellent information, but not a light read.

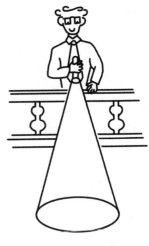

Also in the Good News About Retailing series...

Thriving in the Shadow of Giants and *Raking in the Dough.*

Appendix B
Spotlight on Employee Forms

I use the word "interview" for both write-ups and performance reviews, because it implies a *discussion* between two people. Just like any formal meeting, however, these interviews should be recorded, and the sample forms below can help you do just that. It is advisable to have the employee fill in the answers to questions five and six for the disciplinary write-up. On the review form, I've given you a few examples of criteria that might apply to a salesperson. To develop your own evaluation forms, come up with a separate list of performance criteria for each staff position, based on your written description for that job.

THE EMPLOYEE INTERVIEW FORM (for disciplinary write-ups)

Date _____ Employee Name _____

Department _____ Title _____

1) What is the infraction?

2) What is the course of action needed to correct the situation?

3) Has the employee requested any additional training or support to prevent the infraction from recurring? If so, what?

4) What will be the consequence if the employee repeats the infraction?

5) What is the employee's explanation for the infraction?

6) Does the employee have any other comments?

I have read and understood the above comments. I understand that my signing this form does not necessarily mean that I agree with them.

Employee Signature _____ Date _____

Supervisor Signature _____ Date _____

PERFORMANCE INTERVIEW FORM (for periodical reviews)

Date _____ Employee Name _____

Department _____ Title _____

This review covers the period from _____ to _____.

Section I.: Performance Evaluation

5 = excellent; 4 = very good; 3 = acceptable; 2 = marginal; 1 = unacceptable

Product knowledge	5	4	3	2	1
Ability to sell across product categories	5	4	3	2	1
Understanding of procedures for store's opening and closing	5	4	3	2	1
Participation in subsidized sales training programs	5	4	3	2	1
Adherence to store's dress code	5	4	3	2	1
Punctuality	5	4	3	2	1
Overall Evaluation	5	4	3	2	1

Section II. Career Development

1) How has the employee met the goals set at the previous review?

2) What are the employee's current skills and strengths?

3) What would you like to see the employee work on before the next review?

4) In order to be considered for promotion, the employee should meet the following goals:

Section III. Employee-Supervisor Discussion

1) Employee's comments.

2) Supervisor's comments.

I have read and understood the above three sections. I understand that my signing this form does not necessarily mean that I agree with them.

Employee Signature _____ Date _____

Supervisor Signature _____ Date _____

Index

THE ARMARIUM PRESS.

Scribes and scholars of the ancient world would store a valuable scroll or codex in an *armarium*, the precursor to the modern bookcase. Just as the *armaria* protected those early works of learning, we at The Armarium Press aim to preserve some of the oldest traditions of book publishing.

The small creatures from the woodcut seen on our endpapers stand for speed (the butterfly) and steadfastness (the crab). During the Renaissance, the earliest commercial printers used these and similar symbols to represent the Latin phrase *festina lente*, which we have taken for our motto. Translated as "make haste slowly," these words embody the spirit with which we publish our books.